W9-BAZ-758

## "UNDERSTANDING IS THE FORERUNNER OF CURE."

While you read this, you may be bewildered by what is happening to you. Perhaps the task of facing today seems too much for your tired mind to think about. When I explain to some bewildered, nervously ill people that their suffering is based on nervous fatigue, they are at first dubious that such strange, disturbing symptoms as theirs could have such an apparently simple cause.

But understanding nervous fatigue is the key to understanding the baffling experiences that make recovery from nervous illness so elusive—within grasp one minute, gone the next. So let me guide you, as I have guided so many, to an understanding of nervous fatigue and to recovery from nervous illness.

Bantam Books by Dr. Claire Weekes
Ask your bookseller for the books you have missed

HOPE AND HELP FOR YOUR NERVES
MORE HELP FOR YOUR NERVES
PEACE FROM NERVOUS SUFFERING
SIMPLE, EFFECTIVE TREATMENT OF AGORAPHOBIA

# MORE HELP
# FOR
# YOUR NERVES

### Claire Weekes
### M.B.E., M.B., D.Sc., F.R.A.C.P.

**BANTAM BOOKS**
NEW YORK · TORONTO · LONDON · SYDNEY · AUCKLAND

MORE HELP FOR YOUR NERVES
*A Bantam Book / published by arrangement with
the author*

*PRINTING HISTORY*
*First published in Great Britain in 1984.*
*Bantam edition / March 1987*

*All rights reserved.*
*Copyright © 1984 by Claire Weekes.*
*This book may not be reproduced in whole or in part, by
mimeograph or any other means, without permission.
For information address: Bantam Books, Inc.*

ISBN 0-553-26401-X

*Published simultaneously in the United States and Canada*

---

*Bantam Books are published by Bantam Books, Inc. Its trade-
mark, consisting of the words "Bantam Books" and the por-
trayal of a rooster, is Registered in U.S. Patent and Trademark
Office and in other countries. Marca Registrada. Bantam
Books, Inc., 666 Fifth Avenue, New York, New York 10103.*

---

PRINTED IN THE UNITED STATES OF AMERICA

O        0 9 8 7 6 5 4

*To my sister, Dulcie Maclaren, for her courage and love; to my friends, Joyce Skene Keating, J.P., Irene Appleton, and Steven Reich, for their great effort and devotion to the work; and to the memory of Elizabeth Coleman, who always put obligation before inclination and love and loyalty before all else.*

# Contents

# 1

# Nervous Fatigue

(a)  Muscular Fatigue
(b)  Emotional Fatigue
(c)  Mental Fatigue
(d)  Fatigue of the Spirit

Understanding nervous fatigue is the key to understanding the baffling experiences that make recovery from nervous illness so elusive—within grasp one minute, gone the next. Understanding is the forerunner of cure.

Nervous fatigue can show itself as one or more of four fatigues: muscular, emotional, mental, and a kind of fatigue of the spirit, and these usually develop in this order.

That sounds straightforward enough, yet few people recognize these fatigues in themselves because their development has been so gradual, so insidious. And yet this development follows a consistent pattern that is the basis of much nervous suffering.

Indeed, recognizing fatigue as an important part of their illness can bring such relief to so many that their subsequent recovery can be straightforward and simple. I said simple. I did not say easy.

At this moment, while you read this, you may be bewildered by what is happening to you. Perhaps the task of facing today and tomorrow seems too much for your exhausted body to attempt, too much for your tired mind to think about. And yet it may be only a few months since you could have done that, and much more, easily.

You may have reached the stage where you feel you would rather close your eyes and never open them again than have to open them tomorrow. All this may be so unlike your old self—indeed may seem to be a reversal of that former self—that your bewilderment may be extreme.

When I explain to some bewildered, nervously ill people that their suffering is based on nervous fatigue, they are at first dubious that such strange, disturbing symptoms as theirs, such utter exhaustion, could have such an apparently simple cause. However, once they are convinced, being nervously fatigued seems less frightening than the "mental" illness they were beginning to suspect was theirs. Their picture of mental illness has so many dark, mysterious places.

The difference between nervous fatigue and nervous illness must be explained. A person can suffer from one or all of the four fatigues—muscular, emotional, mental, and "spiritual"—and still, in my opinion, not be nervously ill. It is only when he becomes *afraid of the effects* of fatigue and allows this fear to interfere with his life that I say he has passed from being nervously fatigued to being nervously ill.

Of course there are many different kinds of nervous illness. In this and in my previous books, *Hope and Help for Your Nerves, Peace from Nervous Suffering*, and *Simple, Effective Treatment of Agoraphobia*. I am concerned mainly with the simplest and most common kind: the anxiety state.

Anxiety is closely related to fear. The difference between them is one of timing as well as of intensity. For instance, in an acute emergency—such as facing an immediate danger—we would say we were afraid, whereas

2

when contemplating a threatening future event we would say we were anxious rather than afraid.

The term *anxious* comes from the Latin *anxius* meaning being upset about some future uncertain happening. So, literally, being in an anxiety state should mean being in a condition of prolonged anxiety. However, in practice, a person in an anxiety state is both anxious and afraid and is very often particularly afraid of his nervous symptoms.

I say "particularly afraid of his symptoms" because there are two main types of anxiety state. In the first, the original stress has passed and is no longer responsible for the illness. The sufferer is now concerned with fear of the symptoms this original stress brought. He is afraid of the state he is in, caught in a maze of fear from which he cannot free himself. So his continuing anxiety state is based on fear of symptoms.

In the second type, the sufferer is more concerned with some problem or problems that may have caused his illness and is not cured until these problems are resolved. Peace of mind about his problems is usually essential for his cure.

In my practice the vast majority of people were of the first type. They were afraid of their nervous symptoms and often also of the strange experiences stress brought, and in this book I am mainly concerned with them. However, my teaching about understanding nervous fatigue also helps people with a specific problem or problems (even those with a subconscious cause of illness)—it gives them an understanding of their symptoms and experiences, which at least clears some bewilderment and so opens the way to recovery.

As mentioned earlier, as long as a nervously fatigued person is not unduly anxious about or afraid of his condition, he *is not*, in my opinion, in an anxiety state, not nervously ill.

Regardless of whether a person is nervously ill or merely nervously fatigued, he will benefit from understanding the four fatigues. Even those people who have never suffered from nervous fatigue can be protected from it by understanding it.

So let me guide you, as I have guided so many, to an understanding of nervous fatigue and to recovery from any existing nervous illness.

# (a) MUSCULAR FATIGUE

THE FIRST FATIGUE. Ordinary muscular fatigue is easy to recognize. It may come after strenuous exercise, when it's good to relax—especially in a hot bath—and enjoy the aching muscles that speak so satisfyingly of achievement. However, the muscular fatigue that comes with nervous fatigue is not enjoyable. It comes, not from the extra use of muscles, but from their abuse—from subjecting them to too constant and too severe tension.

Resting muscles are usually in a condition called tone, which is a state balanced between relaxation and contraction; in this way, they are kept ready for use. Tone is maintained by reflex nervous arcs; for example, were you to sit and cross your legs at the knees and tap the crossing leg, just below the kneecap, it would automatically jerk. You couldn't stop this because the action is a reflex; what is more, your leg could jerk that way all day without becoming tired. Reflex action is not tiring. However, *prolonged tension in muscles upsets tone*—the balance between relaxation and contraction— *and also allows the chemicals of fatigue to accumulate. So aching begins.*

This is perhaps the main reason why nervously ill people so often complain of aching legs, aching back, aching neck, and, less frequently, aching arms.

The ache from tension is persistent, and should its victim have to stand, perhaps for only a few minutes, he will look around for support, preferably somewhere to sit, even lie, to relieve those heavy, aching, dragging legs. And yet there is nothing organically wrong with those legs; they are only fatigued through tension.

A feeling of weakness can also follow tension. Bend your right leg at the knee and fiercely tense it. Hold it that way for 30 seconds and then release it. Even after such a short spell of tension, it may feel shaky. The weakness of those shaky legs of nervous fatigue has such simple explanation.

*Blurred vision*. Muscular fatigue can also affect the delicate muscles that accommodate the lens of the eye, so that vision may be blurred, especially on looking quickly from a near to a far object and vice versa. Also, objects in bright sunshine may appear as if in shadow. Although perhaps frightening, these upsets are temporary and unimportant; however, the sufferer with no knowledge of fatigue may think he is going blind and fear further attacks.

*All-over headaches*. Tension in neck and scalp muscles can cause a headache that may extend from above the eyes, over the top of the head, to the base of the skull, and into the neck. There may also be very tender spots over the temples, at the base of the skull and down the sides of the trapezius—the stout muscle that helps support the head and anchor it to the body.

In addition, the head may feel so heavy, or the scalp muscles so sore that resting comfortably on the pillow at night may be difficult without a painkiller. For permanent cure, tension itself must be eased. However, knowing that tension is the cause of the pain (not a brain tumor!) relieves some anxiety and hence some tension.

Much has been written today about removing tension and stress by practicing relaxing exercises. For nervously fatigued and nervously ill people, I recommend such exercise, at first directed by a competent teacher. If this is not practical, I suggest discussion with their doctor.

We can be too anxious about always being relaxed and so may become tenser that usual. I advise relaxing at a set time, once or twice daily, and then worrying no more about it for the rest of the day. Such a daily routine can be built into our subconscious.

Relaxing through subconscious programming is more successful than becoming tense through constantly trying to remember to relax!

How we sit, stand, and lie can be revealing. Trying to support the head in an uncomfortable position—for example, reading in bed or in a chair with an uncomfortable back—tenses head and neck muscles.

Having one's eyes on another job before finishing the one at hand is another guarantee of tension. A whirlwind can propel a toothbrush to finish its job when its owner spots dust on the shelf above the basin. Here again, the subconscious can be harnessed to help. Short, daily, routine practices at moving (cleaning teeth!) slowly will be enough to calm the whirlwind.

Although I mention treatment here, I reserve discussion of further treatment of the four nervous fatigues until the chapter on recovery.

## (b) EMOTIONAL FATIGUE

THE SECOND FATIGUE. If during stress our body always remained calm, we would feel no emotional fatigue, and there would be many fewer sufferers of nervous illness. However, our body doesn't work that way. When nerves are subjected to stress, especially to strong emotions such as fear, for a long time, they can be aroused to record emotion with increasing intensity and often with unusual swiftness. They become trigger-happy and fire off at the slightest provocation. I call this aroused state *sensitization*. Sensitization of nerves is a most important part of nervous fatigue and consequently of nervous illness—of the anxiety state in particular, to which, in my opinion, it is so often an important contributing cause.

When nerves are severely sensitized, emotion—especially fear—can seem to strike with physical force. The sufferer, rarely recognizing this as sensitization, becomes bewildered and afraid of it and so puts himself into a fear-adrenaline-fear cycle. *This is the crucial point where so many people pass from being simply sensitized to becoming nervously ill.*

To understand the fear-adrenaline-fear cycle we should understand how our nervous system works. Although I describe this in earlier books, it is necessary to include a brief description here.

*Fear-adrenaline-fear cycle.* Our nervous system consists of two divisions: voluntary and involuntary. By means of voluntary nerves we move our muscles more or less as we wish. The voluntary nerves are under our direct command—hence their name, voluntary.

The involuntary nerves, with help from our glands, control the functioning of our organs: heart, lungs, bowels, and so on. Unlike the voluntary nerves they, with a few exceptions, are not under our direct control—hence their name, involuntary. However, they respond to and register our moods; for example, when afraid, our cheeks may blanch, our heart race, and our blood pressure rise. We don't consciously do this and—what is so important in understanding nervous illness—we have no power to stop these reactions other than to change our mood. Research workers are experimenting today (for example, with relaxation and meditation) to try to control involuntary reaction; so far their results still depend on calming mood.

The involuntary (sometimes called autonomic) nerves themselves consist of two divisions: sympathetic and parasympathetic. In a peaceful body these two hold each other in check. However, when under stress (for example, when we become angry, afraid, or excited) one division dominates the other. In most people the sympathetic dominates the parasympathetic. These are the people whose heart races, blood pressure rises, and so on. This is called the fight-or-flight response.

Sympathetic nerves are activated by hormones. A

hormone, as defined by *Collins Concise English Dictionary*, is a substance formed in some organ of the body and carried to another organ or tissue, where it has a specific effect. Several hormones are involved in sympathetic reaction to stress, but for the sake of simplicity I will speak only of adrenaline, the best known and perhaps the prime mover of all the hormones released by sympathetic nerves.

Occasionally, under stress, parasympathetic nerves dominate: pulse rate decreases, blood pressure falls. However, more usually the reaction is sympathetic, not parasympathetic, and when I speak of the fear-adrenaline-fear cycle I mean sympathetic reaction.

In my earlier books I called the sympathetic nerves "adrenaline-releasing nerves" and will do so here, because they are certainly not "sympathetic" as we understand that word.

Among his many different symptoms, a sensitized person under stress, as well as feeling his heart beating unusually quickly, may feel it "thump" or "miss" beats; he may have attacks of palpitation and feel his body vibrating with what he may describe as an electrical buzz; feel tremor, muscle jerks, muscle weakness, tingling in his limbs, churning stomach, light-headedness, and so on; and above all, a spasm of fear may be felt as a flash of panic. These symptoms can be so bewildering and upsetting that the sufferer may become more afraid of them than of the cause of his original stress.

Surely it can be understood how, by adding the extra stress of fear to his original stress, the sufferer stimulates the release of more and more adrenaline (and other stress hormones) and so further intensifies the symptoms he dreads, *which are themselves the symptoms of stress*. This is the fear-adrenaline-fear cycle into which a sensitized person can easily be trapped and so placed on the way to nervous fatigue, perhaps nervous illness.

It is easy to add fear of fear when an original spasm of fear is felt as a scorching flash. Naturally the sufferer

8

recoils from the flash and, as he recoils, adds a second flash. I call these two fears first and second fear. Indeed, a sensitized person may be more concerned with his physical feeling of fear (usually panic) than with the original danger that brought it, and because that old bogey sensitization prolongs the first flash, the two fears may feel like one. This is why a sufferer fails to recognize the two separate fears and so fails to see how he prolongs his illness by adding the second fear. He resensitizes himself with every spasm of second fear. For him there is no greater enemy than his lack of understanding.

A nervously ill person may become so afraid of his symptoms that he may avoid places where he thinks stress will bring them. Therefore, he may become afraid to leave the protection of his home. This condition, called agoraphobia, is becoming more widely recognized today. In my opinion, it is no more than *a particular stage* in an anxiety state. I discuss this in detail in my book *Simple, Effective Treatment of Agoraphobia*.

It is important to understand that a person in an anxiety state (whether agoraphobic or not) may have continuous underlying sensitization because he constantly resensitizes himself with anxiety and fear. SENSITIZATION, IN A PERSON WITH NO FEAR OF IT, WOULD HEAL ITSELF.

As mentioned earlier, I stress the importance of sensitization because it is the forerunner of emotional fatigue and therefore possibly also of nervous illness. The sequence is stress (either sudden or gradual), then sensitization, then bewilderment and fear. These are followed eventually by emotional fatigue and the added complications this brings—all possibly appearing finally as nervous illness.

Sensitization is the prime cause of emotional fatigue because, when severe, it exaggerates *all* emotions and so gradually depletes the sufferer's store of emotional energy. Having all emotions exaggerated is bewildering indeed and is one of the main reasons why a sensitized person sometimes thinks he must be going mad. For example, mad. For example, a slightly sad sight can seem tragic; a gloomy sight, overwhelmingly eerie; impatience can be felt as agitation; noise amplified until it seems intolerable; even a moment of joy can be felt hysterically. A sensitized person, feeling emotion as intensely as this, must inevitably become emotionally fatigued and "drained."

A nervously fatigued woman anxiously watched her old mother slump dejectedly as she walked up the garden path to a taxi waiting to take her to her one-room apartment and loneliness. Normally the daughter could have comforted herself with the thought that she would often visit her mother, would take her out, get her to join the Senior Citizens Club, perhaps get her interested in a hobby; but now in her sensitized anguish she could not convince herself of any of this. For her, there seemed only heartbreaking anxiety, and she wondered how long she could survive it.

Another nervously fatigued woman, while sight-seeing in England, visited some Roman baths. These could seem a bit gruesome to anyone, but to her they were so eerie she could hardly restrain herself from running outside. She was bewildered by her strong reaction. I explained that sensitization had exaggerated her feelings and that her agitated revulsion was only an intensified, sensitized version of the normal queasy feeling that anyone could get in the same situation.

*Guilt.* Most of us have some guilt tucked away that we have learned to live with without letting it upset us too much—but not so the sensitized person. Guilt shouts so loudly at him that he feels he will never be reconciled to it. He sees no light at the end of that tunnel. Also, even if he struggles successfully with one guilt, sensitization will soon present him with another. He has only to think of some guilt, perhaps up until now long forgotten, to immediately feel that frightening *whoosh*.

Some therapists say that a patient who comes with a list of guilty worries is "that kind of person"—always looking for something to worry or feel guilty about. He may be, but more likely he is sensitized. Unfortunately, instead of an explanation of sensitization, tranquilizers are too often the only remedy prescribed. Also, some therapists make too much of guilt simply because the patient does; so while the sufferer may take only one or two small guilts to his therapist, he may leave with a heavy bundle.

The impulse to confess guilt is strong while emotional and fatigued; the urge to be relieved of that heavy load on the chest is so insistent. However, a sufferer should beware of yielding to such an urge while sensitized. Confessing guilt can sometimes complicate, not comfort. How essential it is to understand sensitization. I discuss coping with guilt in chapter 3.

*Thunder in the street*. Sensitization can also exaggerate noise. Heavy vehicles can sound like thunder in the street, and sitting through a noisy movie can feel like torture. The person, who does not understand that noise is temporarily amplified by sensitized auditory nerves, is naturally bewildered, and this is increased by the strength of the force that grips and incites him to "rush away from it all."

*Love intensified*. More bewildering still (as if he hasn't had enough already!), even pleasant experiences can be exaggerated; for example, the intensity of the love felt at no more than the sight of a loved one's hand can move the sensitized person to tears.

*Joy felt hysterically*. And, as already mentioned, a rare moment of joy can be felt hysterically. A nervously ill man described how, on one occasion when standing beside a piano while a friend played the accompaniment to a rollicking song, he joined in the singing. When they finished, his friend turned and said, "Don't tell me you're depressed and ill! You sang that better than any of us. You seemed deliriously happy!" The man explained to me, "Doctor, if they only knew! While I was singing I felt more manic than happy. In fact, *delirious* was the right word. That was how I felt. If only I could stay just a little bit happy and not the way I am—way up one minute and down the next. They haven't a clue, doctor!"

*The shock of waking.* A sensitized body can react to the slightest shock. Even the mild shock of waking from sleep can make a heart race. This may be accompanied by such a strong feeling of foreboding that the sufferer may need to keep reassuring himself that nothing terrible has happened or is about to happen.

Such a person, fearing anxiety so intensely, may become so susceptible to it that the mere hint of its approach can grip "the pit of his stomach" with a gnawing ache—and how he longs for a comforting word to ease that ache. Sensitization can be a real stomach gripper!

Also, while he is so responsive to anxious thought, the slightest hazard his imagination may conjure up seems overwhelming; for example, if he tosses at night and cannot sleep, the sensitized person easily imagines he will never be able to sleep properly again. And what a response he gets from his sensitized body!

Because of such flashing response to any anxious thought, he may feel powerless to make decisions, be embarrassingly suggestible, and so become gradually bereft of confidence. At this stage he may feel as if his personality has disintegrated, as if both he and the world are unreal.

We describe some people with exaggerated reactions (not necessarily nervously fatigued or nervously ill) as unbalanced, and a sensitized person certainly feels this way. He may feel this imbalance so acutely that he begins to think he is some sort of weakling. One man said desperately, "I am the exact opposite to what I used to be, to what I really am. What is happening?" He did not understand that this feeling of imbalance was temporary and was no more than his body's sensitized expression of ordinary, normal emotion. Small wonder that one so buffeted by emotion is incredulous when told that his suffering is no more than sensitized nerves exaggerating normal reaction and that when freed from the effects of tension, sensitization can heal itself. This is why understanding sensitization and the part it plays in causing emotional fatigue is so important: UNDERSTANDING IN ITSELF RELEASES SOME TENSION.

The exhaustion following prolonged, exaggerated emotional reaction (especially if accompanied by upsetting physical nervous symptoms: quickly beating heart, "missed" heartbeats, churning stomach, and so on) is especially bewildering because (1) it can seem so incapacitatingly severe and yet be so little related to physical effort and so little relieved by resting and (2) is so difficult to describe and so rarely understood by those who have never felt it, including the family and even doctors.

One nervously ill woman said, "I feel as if my whole body is a 'nothing,' doctor! I haven't the strength to pull it together, and yet my husband keeps saying, 'For God's sake, pull yourself together, Jess! How can you be so tired, when you've done nothing all day?'"

We can survive long periods of stress provided that our glands—principally pituitary and adrenal—can continue to supply essential hormones. The body adapts to stress. However, if adaptation fails (glands become depleted) we pass to the stage of exhaustion. This is why emotional exhaustion—based on glandular depletion—is not appreciably related to physical effort or appreciably helped by rest but is almost miraculously helped by release from emotional suffering and so from stress.

Apathy and depression warn of approaching depletion. First comes apathy. As I say in my book *Hope and Help for Your Nerves*, even to comb his hair can become such an effort that the sufferer begins to look unkempt and no longer cares.

With further depletion, apathy becomes depression. The depression of nervous illness is almost invariably caused by emotional depletion.

The symptoms and experiences I have been describing may sound frightening. However, they are less frightening when one understands the simple pattern of their development and, realizes that recovery lies in reversing that pattern, as I show later. There is no particular bogey, no compelling outside force. There is only a body's natural reaction to stress—and the body will react just as naturally by healing itself when stress is removed. Much stress is removed simply by understanding.

## (c) Mental Fatigue

THE THIRD FATIGUE. The sensitized, fatigued person is naturally concerned about himself, "how he feels," so his anxious thoughts often (sometimes constantly) turn inward. Much anxious introspection brings mental fatigue, just as concentrated study can bring brain fag in a student. Arthur Rubinstein, speaking at the Juilliard School of Music, advised pupils to practice no more than three or four hours a day; any longer, he said, was wasted time because the mind could not absorb it.

When the mind is fresh, thoughts can flit lightly from subject to subject. In a severely mentally fatigued person, thoughts come haltingly and sometimes so slowly that thinking is an effort, almost as if each thought has to be selected and placed individually in the sentence. Speech may therefore be hesitant, even sometimes stuttering.

The sufferer may also become confused and find concentrating and remembering difficult. Forgetting immediate events can be so persistent that the sufferer may suspect he is going prematurely senile.

Talking can be such a strain for a mentally tired person that if he sees a neighbor approaching he will cross the street rather than talk to him. He may sometimes begin a sentence and feel too tired to finish it.

Before he was so mentally tired, he could spend hours on the weekend sitting in the sun, lazily dipping into the newspapers, scarcely thinking at all as time slipped by, but now he watches time consciously, almost

14

every second of it. And how those seconds drag; an hour can seem like eternity to a mentally fatigued person.

Normally we rest our mind during the moments when we look and listen without concentrating too intensely; unimportant thoughts flit so lightly from subject to subject that we are hardly aware of them: the funny design on the new ironing-board cover, the shine on the leaves of the maple tree. However, when mentally fatigued thoughts do not flit, they seem to stick. This is one reason why a mentally tired person gnaws at a worry, feeling unable to release it, especially if the worry holds fear.

When thoughts "stick" and are accompanied by fear, the way is prepared for the development of obsessions and phobias. So many obsessions and phobias *begin in this simple way*.

An obsession is a thought that preoccupies a mind to an abnormal degree, and this is exactly what can happen to a sensitized person suffering from mental fatigue, when a repeated "sticky" thought that frightens comes with such force that it seems to propel its victim almost physically. Surely it is understandable how obsession can be born at this point. Understanding this is extremely important, because with understanding obsession loses its mystery and some of its power to frighten.

A fairly common obsession is doubt about loving one's spouse. A nervously ill woman said that although she knew she really loved her husband, the thought that she didn't kept recurring so frequently and with such force that she was beginning to think it was true. Of course, it was her sensitized response to this fear and its repetition in her tired mind that was convincing her. When sensitization and mental fatigue come together, throwing off frightening thoughts can seem impossible.

This woman found that her inability to disregard her upsetting thoughts, although in her heart she knew them to be false, was one more proof that she was going mad. How many nervously fatigued or nervously ill people have thought this! And, of course, the more frightened she felt, the more sensitized she became, and the more overpowering and persistent were her thoughts.

She admitted that the thought about not loving her husband was most convincing and stuck most tenaciously when she was tired. She also said there were moments when she could see this thought for what it really was: no more than a silly thought in a very tired mind. At such times the idea seemed so absurd that she could smile at it. I call these flashes of normal thinking *glimpsing*. I discuss curing obsession by glimpsing in a later chapter.

A phobia is an irrational, persistent fear. This can develop very simply in a sensitized person. While mental fatigue makes the development more likely, sensitization alone can be enough. A sensitized person, while waiting in a queue, instead of feeling normal exasperation, can feel agitated panic and from then on may avoid standing in any queue, so developing a queue phobia. In this simple way many phobias arise. Understandably simple, isn't it?

*"Muzzy" head.* A mentally fatigued person may say his mind feels enveloped in a blanket, feels dull, heavy, thick. This may be aggravated by blurred vision and perhaps a tendency to stagger slightly (accompanying muscular fatigue). Some say they feel as if a good hard crack on the head would clear it.

In mental fatigue an attack of muzzy head may last from a few hours to days. As one woman described it, "I seem to have a wall in my head that my thoughts knock against. It's very hard to concentrate; before, I always had a very clear head and good insight. But this muzzy head! When it clears I can think very well, but when it descends, I'm finished!

"I had a guilty experience about which I worried so much. I couldn't get worry off my mind. My psychiatrist told me that I was punishing myself and put me on medication. This helped, but this 'thing' came back again. I would have a clear head for half an hour and in that time

16

I could talk, even laugh, and then all of a sudden I would remember the guilt, start crying inwardly, and the muzzy head would descend."

Not recognizing her muzziness as a combination of brain fag and tension, she became alarmed by it, and so added to her problem stress, more tension, more brooding, and therefore more brain fag.

While imprisoned by his blanket of mental fatigue, a sufferer, because of slowed thinking and muzzy head, may become aware of a pressing consciousness of self—especially of his actions and his thoughts. This inward thinking, as I call it, may persist after most of the other symptoms of nervous illness have gone; indeed, it is sometimes the last symptom with which he has to contend.

He rarely recognizes it as that old bogey mental fatigue still at work, binding his mind in the tracks it has been following for the previous months or years. Exasperation at being caught in this trap brings more inward thinking, more stress, more tension—a frightening cycle— and the harder he tries to escape from it, the more bound within it he feels.

This cycle of fatigue and sensitization working together *is following simple, natural laws that can be reversed.* Inward thinking can be cured, as I show later.

*Sudden glare shocks!* A mentally fatigued person, especially when used to the shade and shelter of indoors, can feel sudden shock on opening the front door and facing the light. In my book *Hope and Help for Your Nerves*, I described a mentally fatigued, nervously ill man who was obliged to pass through a dark tunnel before emerging on to a sunlit beach packed with people and gay umbrellas. He was so shocked by the sudden brightness that he felt unreal, like a sleepwalker. The shock arrested his thoughts and gave him insight into the grayness of the world he had been living in—a world of constant anxious introspection— and he *recognized this grayness as no more than persistent mental fatigue*.

The experience helped him recover. For the first time he understood the meaning of mental fatigue and became aware of how absorbingly bound he had been in his own anxious thoughts. He could see now that his trouble was not so much the gravity of his problems as the fatigued state he was in. This came as a revelation because for weeks he had been desperately gnawing at those problems, thinking that they were insoluble. Understanding helped release him.

## (d) FATIGUE OF THE SPIRIT

THE FOURTH FATIGUE. Finally, there is fatigue of the spirit. When a nervously fatigued person is so depleted that every action, perhaps every thought, is an effort, he begins to wonder if the struggle is worth it. Some say they feel as if they have been suddenly precipitated into old age, that they haven't the strength to face another day, let alone weeks or months. The will to survive falters, especially if the sufferer has been trying to recover by fighting his way out of fatigue. The best way to increase fatigue is to try to fight it, as I will show in the next chapters.

First, the fatigued spirit must somehow find fresh hope and courage. The merest glimmer is enough to begin with. It may have to be, because even that can seem too much for an exhausted spirit to resurrect. However, recovery can build on such a slender foundation, so slender that at the slightest puff of discouragement it may seem to collapse.

And yet, if there is understanding and a plan for recovery instead of a hopeless no-man's-land, hope and courage do grow again, as bravely as the green shoots grow on the burnt-out tree stumps in a forest ravaged by fire. I have seen so many people take those first shaky steps to recovery holding desperately on to such slender hope and courage, sustained by the understanding I have been privileged to give them.

Although those first steps may seem weak and faltering, they hold the same indomitable strength that has carried us all through millions of years of our evolutionary struggle. We all have this strength, this power, within us, and it will work miracles if we trust it to help us learn to walk and live with fear, so that we can eventually walk and live without fear.

So, on, brave spirit.

# 2

# Recovery

(a)  Facing
(b)  Accepting
(c)  Floating
(d)  Letting Time Pass

It may be difficult for a sufferer from nervous fatigue to appreciate the difference between his fatigue and nervous illness. Some—particularly executives struggling to hold down an important and stressful job, indeed anyone trying to do a day's work that seems beyond their ability to cope—may suspect that, if not already suffering from nervous illness, they are at least threatened by it. So they have two struggles, one with their fatigue and another with their fear of it becoming illness. This struggle is particularly poignant because in their exhausted state their fear of nervous illness can open the door to it.

Understanding his symptoms and experience will at least relieve the nervously fatigued person of bewilderment. Also, with understanding, he is less likely to become afraid of "the state he is in" and, although perhaps tottering with fatigue, can keep himself free from actual nervous illness.

However, if fear, through ignorance, takes control, the fatigued person often flounders in despair, almost blindly reaching for help. At this time the right guidance is crucial. Many years of experience in helping hundreds of nervously fatigued and nervously ill people have proved that the guidance I now offer, if followed, will bring peace.

I teach recovery from nervous fatigue and nervous illness by using four simple concepts: facing, accepting, floating, and letting time pass. Although I have discussed these in previous books, many readers have continued to ask questions about them; so I will discuss them here in further detail.

It becomes confusing to talk about nervously fatigued and nervously ill people and at the same time try to differentiate between them. So henceforth I will speak to the nervously ill, although stressing that much of the advice given applies equally to the nervously fatigued.

## (a) FACING

Facing means acknowledging that cure must come from inside you—guidance and help from outside, of course, but fundamentally by your effort—and this means by your facing the things you fear. RECOVERY LIES IN THE PLACES AND EXPERIENCES FEARED.

Facing also means not shying away from nervous symptoms *for fear of making them worse*. Shying away is running away, not facing.

Recently I met a striking example of not facing in a Canadian who panicked when away from home and who was consequently afraid to travel any distance from home, either alone or accompanied. His therapist encouraged him to go out as far as he could without panicking. If he panicked (and he surely would), he was told to return home and repeat the journey later, still going only as far as he could with comfort. The therapist's aim was for the patient to become so used to that particular journey that he could eventually make it without panic.

This man managed so well that he decided to spend his holiday in the United States. He spent two weeks in Las Vegas and did not panic. He returned home in triumph.

The next day he went down to his bank, the same bank he had visited so often when ill. He stood on the old familiar spot in the queue, and as he handed his bankbook to the same teller, the one with the thick glasses, memory smote and he panicked. *And this time it was a smasher*, because with the return of panic came despair. He had managed so well before going away, and yet all he need do now was simply stand in the queue in his own bank for panic to sweep once more. No wonder he despaired and thought, "What can I do *now*?" He was desolate.

He had found peace only by "getting-used-to." He had never faced panic, had never learned how to cope with it fully. He had been taught to avoid it, to try to quiet it, never how to pass through it until *it no longer mattered*.

It is true that some people feel they have been helped by avoiding, but *they are vulnerable to returns of panic*. At the return of even a slight spasm, their brave little flag can crumple.

I stress again and again that in place of an inner voice that says hopefully, "Perhaps it won't happen here," there must be a supporting voice that says, "It doesn't matter if it *does* happen here. It just doesn't matter any more. You can cope with it!" The voice that says, "Perhaps it won't...?" is the sword of Damocles, waiting.

While I never teach the "getting-used-to" technique to people afraid of traveling away from home (called agoraphobic), it has its place in treating people with specific phobias, such as fear of cats, thunderstorms, heights, and so on. Behaviorists build a program of graduated exposure to a feared object that can not only relieve but often cure this kind of phobia.

Also, it is possible to get so used to some nervous symptoms that they no longer matter. Then without the stress of mattering, they may, of course, calm, even disappear.

I also said facing means accepting that cure must

come from within oneself and not from some permanent outside crutch. This means recognizing that the way to recovery can be difficult. A journalist wrote in a magazine that she had been agoraphobic for years but could now go anywhere provided she took a special tablet three times a day. "Now," she wrote, "I have only to come off the tablets and I am cured!" She had only to stop taking tranquilizers! In other words, while still lame, she had only to throw away her crutches and walk.

Whether she could do this would depend on her luck the first time she tried to go out without her tablets. If she was confident and stayed confident, all could be well, but she needed only a slight shiver of doubt for panic to strike and all could be lost. This applies to the return of all the symptoms of nervous illness when tranquilized away. Tranquilization merely postpones the time when symptoms must be faced to be cured. There is a place for tranquilization, but it should be chosen with discretion. I talk more about this later.

The permanent cure of nervous illness based on fear of symptoms and experiences—as so much nervous illness is—begins by facing fear itself, especially at the peak of its intensity, THE RIGHT WAY.

While facing fear blindly is brave, it is too often futile and exhausting. For recovery, the sufferer must be shown how to face fear *by accepting, floating,* and *letting time pass.*

## (b) ACCEPTING

After becoming prepared to face, the next step is acceptance, and because acceptance is the key to recovery, we should be sure of its meaning. Acceptance means letting the body loosen as much as possible and then going toward, not withdrawing from, the feared symptoms, the feared experiences. It means "letting go," "going with," bending like the willow before the wind—rolling with the punches!

When one goes forward this way into panic (into *any* of the feared symptoms), the secretion of the hormones (principally adrenaline) producing the symptoms is reduced. Even if only slightly, *it is reduced*. On the other hand, tense withdrawal encourages further secretion and more sensitization and, therefore, more intense symptoms.

While at first acceptance of physical symptoms, especially panic, may seem impossible, practicing thinking about acceptance is always possible, and this alone can release some tension (although perhaps only a microscopic amount to begin with), so that when "it" comes to do its worst, the worst is tempered. If you stand taut and say bravely with clenched teeth, "Come and do your worst! But get it over quickly!" you are only "putting-up-with."

A patient will complain that he has accepted but that the dreaded symptoms are still there. "I have accepted the churning in my stomach, but I still have it! So what do I do now?" How could he have accepted, while he still complained about it?

The most frightening symptom is panic because, in a sensitized person, it can strike so fiercely and so quickly that merely thinking about it apprehensively can bring it on. The natural reaction is to recoil, to tense against it, to try to stop the flash from coming; however, tension brings more sensitization and so, more panic. Acceptance is a definite physiological process that eventually soothes. I say eventually, because the soothing can rarely be felt immediately. Acceptance is the beginning. Established sensitization can rarely be soothed quickly, because it takes time for the new mood of acceptance to be felt as peace.

Although the symptoms of nervous illness are always the expression of mood, they are not always an expression of the present mood. When acceptance is first practiced, the body may still be registering the tense, frightened mood of the preceding weeks, months and years and may continue to do this (but with progressively reduced intensity) even after the mood of acceptance is established.

This is why nervous illness can be so puzzling. A

nervously ill person may begin to accept, but when the symptoms do not quickly disappear, he loses heart and becomes apprehensive once more, although trying to convince himself that he is still accepting.

I repeat, it takes time for a body to establish acceptance and for this to bring peace, just as it takes time for fear to be established as continuous tension and anxiety. This is why letting time pass, the last of my four concepts, is so important in treatment.

Understanding makes acceptance so much easier. It is unnecessarily difficult to accept erratic heartbeats if the victim believes that his heart is diseased. How much easier when he understands that the unevenness of those beats is no more than a temporary and unimportant upset in their nervous timing.

Adequate explanation is indeed a boon to the patient preparing to accept. However, it is not always given. One woman said, "I can't describe how I feel. I just feel funny. The doctors just look at me and give no explanation!" "Feeling funny" can be an accurate description of how a nervously ill person does sometimes feel, and describing his "funny" symptoms can be difficult, because symptoms of fatigue and anxiety when working together can be vague and undefined, and vague symptoms can be just as upsetting as more definite ones.

If you feel like this, provided your doctor has examined you and said that your "funny" symptoms are nervous, accept them and be comforted to know that such feelings are common in nervous illness and never important. Blind acceptance can cure as well as acceptance based on knowledge; but when knowledge guides, acceptance is easier.

Some doctors, while knowing that "funny" symptoms are "nervous," do not understand their physiology and so cannot explain them. So, while "funny" nervous feelings should be accepted without full explanation (if none is available), explanation of more definite symptoms (weakness, trembling, headache, palpitations, difficulty in swallowing, and so on) should be sought. I explain these in detail in my first book, *Hope and Help for Your Nerves*.

Don't think I use the word *acceptance* lightly. I know what I am asking. It's not easy to accept the fire that consumes; not easy to work with the fire burning. It's not easy to accept and work with a body that feels as if it is vibrating or shaking; with stomach churning, limbs aching, heart pounding, sight blurred, head swimming—I'm making it sound terrible, aren't I? It can be terrible, and it is made worse if the mind, at the same time, feels as if it is drawn out into a frail thread that will snap with the slightest extra tension. I understand all this, but I still preach acceptance.

Recently a woman phoned to say that that morning had been especially rough for her. She'd come through by saying to herself, "I'll be talking to Dr. Weekes in a couple of hours. I'll have some peace then!" The thought of the peace to come sustained her. But living for such peaceful moments was not good enough; it meant that she would make little progress. There is no lasting peace in waiting for someone else to bring it. Such relief from suffering is only a respite.

I explained to this woman that peace lay within herself and depended on her attitude when the symptoms were at their fiercest, and that that was the moment for her to practice the acceptance that would help her find lasting peace.

She thought for a while and then said, "You mean I have to find the eye of the hurricane?" She had the message at last. Sailors say that at the center of the hurricane there is a place of peace, which they call the eye. The storm swirls around but cannot reach it. To find it the ship must first go through the storm.

If that woman were to work as willingly as possible, accepting the symptoms (the hurricane) and *not adding second fear*, she would find the eye of the storm herself, and although the symptoms might at first seem as fierce as ever, there would be some peace and reassurance in knowing that she was on the right course at last, without having to wait for the doctor's soothing words.

Peace of mind built on earned confidence lies not in the absence of symptoms but in their midst, and it is only when one discovers this that the intensity of symptoms abates and there is peace. The process, of course is gradual. The next day the woman reported that while feeling "ghastly" she had sat at her work (she was an artist) and had painted for two hours. For the first time for months she was able to lose herself in the work, while the hurricane raged within. For once, the hurricane did not seem so important.

It takes courage to face the storm and let happen what will. That woman had been shrinking from the way she felt for 20 years and was still ill. Surely it was time she tried another approach, tried to go into the storm, accepting it willingly—well, as willingly as she could manage at first.

Many are helped by understanding that the flash of panic is no more than an electric discharge, that while it may feel devastating, it is only an electrical discharge along sensory nerves. SO MANY PEOPLE ALLOW AN ELECTRIC FLASH TO SPOIL THEIR LIVES BY WITHDRAWING FROM IT IN FEAR.

As I have explained so often, fearful withdrawal produces the hormones that stoke the fire of panic. Facing and relaxing toward, with acceptance, help to dampen the flow and eventually stop it.

A sensitized, bewildered person, feeling his panic grow stronger as his sensitization increases, may imagine being flooded by an irresistible tidal wave of panic.

He should understand that there is a limit to the severity of even his panic. If he analyzes his fiercest flash—the flash he thinks too fierce to bear—he will find that at its peak, *he is shudderingly withdrawing from it*.

WHENEVER HE FEARS PANIC HE CAN EVENTUALLY QUELL IT ONLY BY GOING FORWARD INTO IT, NEVER BY WITHDRAWING FROM IT.

A person sustained by this knowledge will one day be surprised by feeling panic sweep over him and yet FEEL ALOOF FROM IT, as if looking down on it. HE HAS LOST HIS fear of panic. We talk about "rising above a situation"; there is no better example.

When there is no longer fear of panic, it gradually subsides. Time becomes the healer. I stress again and again that cure lies in *losing* fear and that this is earned only by learning how to go through it the right way—with acceptance. With such understanding, it is possible to be cured immediately. I have seen this—but, of course, rarely.

Repeated panics can be exhausting. This is when I advise moderate and temporary tranquilization and an occasional rest, on sedation, to help the sufferer regain strength and refresh his spirit. Tranquilization must always be planned so that the sufferer still earns his inner supporting voice born from having faced and accepted.

I talk so much about panic because I am using it as an example from a hierarchy of nervous symptoms: palpitations, churning stomach, trembling hands, and so on. When the sufferer learns to accept these without adding second fear, they also gradually subside. They must, because they too are the symptoms of fear.

You may ask, "But what if the nervously ill person is kept constantly stressed, perhaps frightened, by some problem—perhaps an upsetting domestic situation that is difficult to change? How can accepting the nervous symptoms help him? It can't solve the problem!"

It can't. However, people who develop nervous symptoms because of the stress brought by a problem can also be further upset by the symptoms themselves; the iron-band headache, extreme fatigue, quickly beating heart, sweating hands, and so on. Surely, understanding the nature of these symptoms helps lessen fear of them and so gives greater opportunity to concentrate on trying to solve any problem.

If you are reading this because you are nervously ill, I want you to practice acceptance now. Make yourself comfortable, take a deep breath, let it out slowly, let your tummy muscles sag, give way, and try to feel a willingness to accept. Try to feel this in the pit of your stomach. Practice now.

Did you have a fleeting feeling of acceptance? If you did, you felt the birth of recovery. Continued acceptance will gradually finish the job.

It is necessary to understand the difference between true acceptance and putting-up-with. Putting-up-with (although calling for much bravery) means resistance. It means advancing and retreating at the same time. As I said earlier, it is an attitude of "Hurry! Come quickly and get it over with!" True acceptance means facing and relaxing, being prepared to go slowly with as little self-induced agitation as possible. It is submission.

I have used acceptance again and again in writing and recordings. You may think I place too much importance on it. How could I when it is the key to recovery?

I have said so often that peace lies on the other side of panic: now I shout it. By going through panic to the other side you earn the little voice that says, "It doesn't matter any more if panic comes!" This is the only voice to listen to. It is your staff and will always come to your help in setbacks, even if you find yourself almost helpless on the floor. As it lifts you up, you will feel again that the dreaded bogey no longer matters. As this realization strengthens, courage returns, and you once more find the confidence to practice utter, utter acceptance—perhaps even more willingly.

Acceptance means throwing away the gun and letting the tiger come if he wants to. It sounds terrible, doesn't it? Incredible that cure can lie in such a dangerous procedure; but it does.

Just as facing and accepting are closely related, so are acceptance and floating. Indeed, they are so close that sometimes distinguishing between them is difficult.

Let us now examine floating.

## (c) FLOATING

In the past, orthodox psychiatric treatment rarely recognized the importance of fear of fear and too often persisted with searching for childhood causes, which was neither necessary nor helpful.

One woman wrote, "Not one psychiatrist or psychologist I visited would listen to the validity of the 'fear of the fear' and yet I am living proof of it. They were like stone, and you can't reason with stone."

So, disappointed and confused, perhaps made apathetic with heavy medication, nervously ill people often abandon treatment and, with little hope, sink further into their illness. Some try to treat themselves.

Unfortunately, self-treatment often fails because instinct too readily leads the sufferer in the wrong direction. He tries to *fight* his illness. HE SHOULD FLOAT, NOT FIGHT.

Many ask, "What do you mean exactly by floating, doctor?" I can explain best by giving examples. A nervously sensitized person can become so supertensed with fear that he may stand immobilized, rigid, feeling unable to take another step forward, whether trying to walk along a street, enter a shop, or simply go from room to room at home. He rarely recognizes this "paralysis" as supertension. Indeed, *his instinct is to tense himself still further and try to force his way forward*.

Forcing means more tension and therefore more rigidity. In his despair he may add panic to panic, and when he does, his thoughts may seem to recede (they may actually seem to squeeze up into the back of his head) and become "frozen" until further thought seems impossible. His "brain goes numb." Agoraphobic people know and dread this moment of rigid "paralysis" when trying to move away from home, and fear of it has helped to keep thousands housebound for years.

If the "paralyzed" sufferer, instead of forcing, were to let his body go as slack as possible (and actually feel as if it was sagging), then take a deep breath and exhale slowly while imagining himself *floating forward* without resistance—almost as if floating on a cloud or on water—he would release enough tension to loosen muscles and would be

30

able to move forward, although maybe at first shakily, haltingly.

Another example of floating: a nervously ill person may wake in the morning feeling so tired that he shrinks at the thought of the effort of getting out of bed, dressing, eating—indeed, of doing anything.

He may try to "pull himself together" and this may seem so impossible that he sinks, defeated, back onto the bed. One woman said she felt like an ant looking at Everest.

Instead of seeing only grim effort ahead, she should think, "Okay, I'll make the effort *as gently as I can*. I'll go with it.' I'll try to make no tense effort; I'll submit to it all, let it all happen. I'm not going to fight my way through any of it. I'll stop struggling and try to let my body float up out of it. I'll even float my clothes on."

Can you appreciate the difference here between fighting and floating? Floating means no grim determination, no clenched teeth, and as little "pushing" or forcing as possible.

You may say, "Floating is only relaxing!" It is certainly relaxing, but it is more than that; it is relaxing *with action*. One faces, relaxes, and then floats on through.

Floating does not mean lying and gazing at the ceiling and thinking, "I don't have to make any effort; I'll give up the struggle. I'll just lie here on the bed forever and do nothing!" That's relaxing all right! But it's not relaxing with action. And yet *temporarily* "doing nothing about it" can have a beneficial, refreshing effect—but only temporarily.

The sufferer practicing letting his body float up from his fatigue has no need to search for a way to recovery. It is as if he steps aside from his body and lets it find its own way out of the maze. The body that so skillfully heals a physical wound without our direction can also heal sensitized nerves if given a chance and not hindered by inquisitive fingers picking at the scar. Float, don't pick.

Too often the same difficulties arise again and again in

31

nervous illness, and the repeated effort of fighting the same battle can make the sufferer feel too dispirited to go on searching for a way out. WHERE FIGHTING IS EXHAUSTING, FLOATING—BY REMOVING THE TENSION OF FORCING—MAKES REPEATED EFFORT LESS DAUNTING.

If, when learning to float, loosening a tense body seems impossible, the supertensed person can at least *imagine* himself loosening. Even this works.

As I have already mentioned, people in an anxiety state can be grouped into those who have a special problem or problems causing illness and keeping them ill and those whose only problem is finding a way to recovery from their distressing nervous state.

Those with a specific problem are not expected to float past it, although I have been quoted as having asked this of them. Expecting a bewildered, confused person to find his own answers to his problem is rarely good therapy. It can mean an unnecessarily long period of suffering, because too often, through sensitization and fatigue, the sufferer switches too easily and too quickly from one point of view to another. Holding one point of view that brings some peace is essential for recovery. A good therapist helps his patient find such a viewpoint.

It is rare to meet a nervously ill person who can float past an agitating problem and worry no more about it. I did say in my first book, *Hope and Help for Your Nerves*, "try to let all disturbing, obstructive thought float away, out of your head," but, of course, success here depends on the magnitude of the troublesome thought. When I gave that advice previously, I referred to floating past one's own destructive suggestion. I did not mean the nervously ill should try to float past real problems.

This is one patient's experience of facing, accepting, and floating: "I feel I must write and tell you of the progress I have made this year. For 20 years, since my first attack of panic, I have been agoraphobic. During all these years, at the sight, or mere mention, of the word *bus*, my stomach would turn over, and the idea of getting on one—impossible!

"As you know, last year I got your cassette *Going on Holiday* (your records are worn thin with playing). As a result of constantly listening to the cassette, I decided to face a short cruise for myself and family.

"This year I booked a much longer cruise (a month!) to the Canary Islands. So it was on with the cassette again. The first four days were not so good. The sea was rough, and there was a strong wind. However, I had made up my mind to do everything I have been unable to do for so long. I went six times in the coach to the restaurant *alone*. I went up the mountains at Tenerife, 4,000 feet, with a sheer drop on either side. I even crossed to the shore by launch.

"Only one evening was spoiled. When I entered the dining room that night, I had a terrible feeling of self-consciousness. I just couldn't swallow, and it was my favorite meal, roast turkey! I did the only thing I could think of: I ate the soft vegetables and the dessert and kept repeating to myself, 'Loosen your body! Accept and float! Accept and float!' By the time we had reached the coffee I was floating fine."

So now practice floating, and while you do be prepared to obey the next section and let time pass.

## (d) LETTING TIME PASS

Recovery, like all healing, must be given time. Understandably, the nervously ill person is impatient with time and wants immediate appeasement; but impatience means tension, and tension is the enemy of healing.

The sufferer removes a big obstacle to recovery when he understands that sensitization is a chemical process and needs time for chemical readjustment. A still sensitized body can be deceptively calm in a calm atmosphere, but a body even only slightly sensitized cannot always maintain calmness when under renewed stress. So time, more time, must pass. Time itself is a healer. It's rather like the donkey and the carrot. The carrot (recovery) must be shifted just a little further forward during each setback but always remain within sight.

I am often asked how long recovery will take. So much depends on the degree of sensitization and the circumstances of recovery. There may be constant strain, for example, trying to recover while living with an upsetting domestic situation. Also, it takes time to blunt memory's cutting edge. We can't anesthetize memory. Indeed, when surprised by some grueling memory, who can suppress an inner shudder? And yet the person trying to recover from nervous illness seems to think he should. He wants the balm of constant peace.

It is difficult to understand that a body's sensitized reaction to memory is no more than the working of a natural law, difficult to understand that a setback is not always a setback in the sense that it sets *back* but should be even expected and accepted *as part of recovery*. Its victim is much more likely to believe that some strange jinx is bugging him. His jinx is his lack of understanding. When so close to past upsetting experiences, and with a body still tuned to give a too quick, too intense, reaction to memory's prodding, it is natural to be too easily bluffed by memory into thinking he will never recover.

When memory first strikes it is as if the sufferer has learned nothing from past experience. The symptoms he'd learned to disregard suddenly begin to matter again—very much. And before he has time to study himself enough to think clearly, he feels sucked willy-nilly into the whirlpool of setback. However, if he had originally worked his way out of suffering the hard way—by having truly faced and lived with his symptoms while accepting them, having conquered adding second fear (fear of symptoms, especially fear of panic)—then memory of his original recovery gradually awakens the little inner voice that says, "You've come out of it before. You can do it now! You know that these symptoms do not really matter!" He hears this voice with thanksgiving and relief, because with it comes a special feeling, a realization that the symptoms really do *not* matter. He now *feels* this; he doesn't just *think* it as he did at the beginning of setback. *He now feels it with relief*. Fear gradually goes; relaxation and peace come. He is on the way to true recovery. Recovery is built on *repeated* experiences of discovering that symptoms no longer matter.

When enough setbacks bring enough such experiences, the feeling of symptoms no longer mattering comes more quickly, is more forceful, and the impact of memory's shock becomes weaker and weaker until it is but an echo of former suffering.

It is possibly because memory can shock by bringing back old symptoms so vividly that some therapists speak pessimistically about complete recovery. Indeed, they do not recognize that setback is one of the best teachers and an almost essential halting place in recovery because it gives more time to relearn and practice. Not understanding this, they fail to prepare their patients optimistically for possible setback.

At some point in nervous illness the sufferer may be so ill he no longer cares what happens; however, as he begins to recover, caring returns, and this may be complicated by his feeling that, although much better, he cannot face the future demands and responsibilities of normal living. At such a time he is often accused of "not wanting to get better." Make no mistake: he wants to recover, but at the same time the prospect of coping with the demands of recovery may be so frightening while he is in his present state of only partial recovery that he almost convinces himself that the criticism may be true—another bewilderment in nervous illness!

Enough time must pass to provide a protective layer of normal responses to help him gradually find his balance in normal living, to take normal reaction for granted.

As his body strengthens, his spirits rise, and optimism and confidence return. The process may be so gradual he may be unaware of it. As I said in *Hope and Help for Your Nerves,* "It is this gradualness that makes all possible and only the passage of enough time can bring such gradualness."

A Dutchman once said to Vera Brittain (an English author) that the postwar Dutch were suffering from a spiritual sickness that time and understanding alone would heal. He said that suffering could not be erased the moment the war ended and peace came; time was necessary for the Dutch to regain their balance, their ability to be on top of events, including their own lives. He added, "Be patient with us. We have to grow into liberty." And so must the nervously ill person grow into recovery. There is no electric switch, no overnight cure.

When the sufferer is beginning to recover, he is not only vulnerable to memory but also particularly vulnerable to the tricks any remaining fatigue may play. For example, distinguishing between normal fatigue and some remnant of nervous fatigue can baffle. The sufferer is apt to mistake any fatigue as nervous and jump to the upsetting conclusion that recovery is further away than he had thought. One woman, although much better, was so apprehensively suggestible that when she made foolish mistakes playing bridge, she always blamed lingering illness and became worried. But she had made foolish mistakes at bridge before she was ill! Many nervously ill people expect recovery to bring a state of peace they never previously felt.

As already mentioned, for many people peace is often further delayed by their too fearful, and too tense, recoil from a binding awareness of self—the result of months, even years, of concentration on themselves and their illness. They delay their own recovery by trying to force forgetfulness. *Nothing can be forced in nervous illness.* The only way to lose consciousness of self is to accept it, to accept any thought that comes as part of ordinary thinking. This means that they should think about themselves and their illness *as much as the habit demands* and realize that *it is only a habit fostered by mental fatigue*. Once more I stress that the (key) to recovery is not in *forgetting* but in *no-longer-mattering*, and for this *time* must pass.

When the patient realizes that the intensity of his reaction is part of his sensitization and that if he accepts it and lets more time pass those reactions will gradually become normal, then intense reaction can be borne more philosophically. This is sometimes called regaining one's balance, and, as the Dutchman said to Vera Brittain, it takes time.

# 3

# Some Bewilderments Cleared Away

Over the last 20 years I have been treating nervously ill men and women in Australia, the United Kingdom, and Canada, and the United States by remote control: recordings and regular journals in addition to my books. Some of the journals are included in chapter 4.

Recently I asked some of these people if they had any further questions. I discuss these here and in chapter 5.

**Feeling like passing out while washing up at the sink.** "When I get up in the morning I'm fine for a while and then, when I stand at the sink washing up, I get the feeling of being about to pass out. My head gets tight and hot, my eyes won't focus properly, and my neck tightens. Of course I take a tablet, although I always vow I won't."

Sometimes a man or woman may feel comparatively well on rising, and then the sight of some familiar thing (for the woman quoted above, a sink full of dishes!) rings memory's bell and it tolls, "Look out! You always feel faint here, remember? Watch out you don't fall! You could, you know!"

So stress comes and with it tension: neck muscles contract; the head feels strange, light; eye muscles contract— the lens of the eye will not accommodate and sight is

38

blurred. All because memory rang that wretched bell and tensed a body all too easily tensed.

Of course, with lightheadedness comes fear of fainting, and although this woman says she's never actually fainted, she quickly presents herself with, "What if?" So, more tension, more lightheadedness, more defeat, and probably poorly washed dishes. She wonders, "Could there be something really wrong with my eyes? Am I going blind? And my neck...?" When she begins to doubt, on comes more fear and the bind of extra tension. If only more doctors would explain symptoms more fully to patients whom they think neurotic, they would be surprised by the improvement in the patients.

If only this woman could understand how memory works and think, "What the heck! I can still manage to wash up even though I'm lightheaded. I'm not going blind. My eye muscles will recover when I relax—anyhow, I can still wash up! So here goes!" How different she'd soon feel.

I'm not saying that the symptoms would all go quickly away—they may not; but what a boost to her confidence to be able to work on, lightheaded or not. And confidence brings relaxation and strength, so it wouldn't be long before she no longer noticed any lightheadedness or blurred vision.

A good exercise for this woman would be to stand at the sink and see if she could make her symptoms more severe, even try to "pass out"—this "passing out" is not as easy as she thinks. When she faces her symptoms this way and is finally prepared to accept and work with them, there will be no need for a tablet, and in time the sink will be once more only a sink.

**Joining the world again.** "Your down-to-earth approach I find so helpful. You really do understand us. I have been receiving treatment from a young, well-meaning psychologist, and although he was telling me to keep going out, he gave me no incentive to get going. He has been telling me that I have been hanging on to agoraphobia to keep me dependent on my daughter.

"I can't understand this, because it's wonderful to be able to do things on my own and not have to ask my daughter to come with me.

"At last, with your help, after being shut in and depressed for weeks, I am walking into supermarkets, doing Christmas shopping. I'm part of life. After giving up a stressful job six months ago, I followed your advice and applied for a job as an assistant in a newspaper shop near home for a couple of hours a day. They took me on and, of course, I started worrying that I couldn't do it. My legs were like jelly, and my hands were shaking. I put on a bright smile and thought, 'So what! They're not worried about me. I don't look any different.' And I must say that, although feeling exhausted, by the end of the week I was so happy to collect that pay envelope.

"Another landmark was sitting through a church service. I hadn't been able to do this for a long time. I was up in the balcony, which made things worse, and I thought of all the people I'd have to pass if I wanted to go out. I felt uncomfortable after about an hour and took my coat off; but the panic didn't increase, although looking down made me feel quite dizzy. I just looked around and thought, 'For all I know there could be someone else here feeling like this!' I must say it was with some relief that I sang the last hymn. I felt as if I'd joined the world again."

**Rather weedy creatures?** "I resent the implication that I am a neurotic who can't cope in frightening or tense situations. I cope although frightened, which, of course, makes coping even more difficult. Am I not just a victim of particular circumstances, not a lesser human being? Or am I, as I so often feel, a rather weedy creature who should have learned to be tougher?"

Most nervously ill people have been victims of particular circumstances. I quote a passage from Vicki Baume's autobiography: "I know what I'm worth. . . . There are certain regions of fears in every one of us balanced by certain regions of courage. We are all constructed alike—50 percent hero, 50 percent coward. As for myself, I am, and always was, a coward about noise and speed; I'm also frankly afraid of most mechanical contraptions including the telephone and the Mixmaster. They don't like me either, and they could explode, couldn't they? Definitely I am a misfit for here and today." (Vicki Baume was nearly 70 when she wrote this.) "On the other hand, I bear up fairly well; I'm not afraid of the dark, of being left alone in the house, or of burglars, or of murderers and monsters— not a bit, if that doesn't sound too pompous." She then goes on to say, "My next great fear came in summer with the boom and hiss noise and flash of the fireworks and the hollering crowds on the Kaiser's birthday celebrations. I suppose this is where the fear of noise lodged in my bones and nerves."

I liked her saying that we were 50 percent coward and 50 percent brave. I think we are. Maybe some of us are more afraid than others, some braver; but most of us belong to the 50/50 club.

We should not feel lesser human beings because we happen to be afraid in certain situations. Coping although frightened is true courage. As for being a weedy creature who should have learned to be tougher, with a lot of practice in situations that frighten, we learn to be tougher, but this simply means learning how to cope with nervous reactions. It's as simple as that. When George Bernard Shaw was asked to take the chair at a British Association meeting, St. John Irvine, who was present, said that Bernard Shaw's hand trembled so much with nervousness he could hardly sign the minutes.

Here again, acceptance and practice worked wonders. To quote St. John Irvine again, nine years later Bernard Shaw was able to address the British Association with great aplomb.

Also, being at peace doesn't always mean having a peaceful body. We can be at peace while accepting an old

41

rattling body. Indeed, peace comes because we are *accepting while the body is rattling*. However, even with acceptance and practice, some of us may never know a completely calm body when under stress. The few who say they do are very lucky. Most of us have to work with the symptoms of stress present. I'd say we're all rather brave, not weedy, wouldn't you?

**Obsession.** A person tortured by an obsession is in my experience always capable of understanding—if only fleetingly—the truth about it. For example, a woman obsessed with the belief that her house was contaminated with germs could glimpse the truth while I explained to her that there were few dangerous germs present in any house. I had cultures made from smears taken from each of her rooms, from her refrigerator, tap water, around her drain pipes, and so on, and they were all negative.

When she saw these results she realized that her repeated cleaning (the refrigerator sometimes three times in one day!) was unnecessary.

Yet, as soon as she left me, her reaction to the thought of germs returned so strongly that she was once more caught up in the obsession.

That fleeting moment, when she saw the truth behind her obsession, I call "glimpsing." I cure patients of obsession by teaching them to practice glimpsing regularly and often. To do this, they sit quietly (or stand; it doesn't really matter), think about their obsession, and try to feel all the associated fear; then, while flooded in fear, *at that very moment*, to try to glimpse the truth behind the obsession, or simply to glimpse another point of view.

In the beginning, a mentally tired person (an obsession adds more fatigue to an already tired mind) may be able to glimpse only once or twice daily, but even one quick glimpse of the truth can expose the tricks that mental fatigue is playing and show that physical reaction to the obsession is severe because of sensitization (the constant tension from obsession can be very sensitizing) and not because of the importance or truth of the thought.

I have cured obsessions this way in people who have had years of unsuccessful orthodox treatment, including psychoanalysis, sedation, intravenous injection (e.g., Anafranil), narcoanalysis, electroconvulsive treatment (shock), hypnosis, group therapy, and so on.

One woman, having had various treatments at a local psychiatric hospital over a period of nine years, was described to me in 1975 by her therapist as incurable. Later, at the same hospital, lobotomy was suggested. She refused.

I taught her to glimpse and she cured herself.

In November 1979 (after lobotomy had been refused and she had begun practicing glimpsing) she wrote: "The work you have done has been special. If it weren't for you a lot of us just wouldn't be here today, let alone happy to be here. You ask me if I have any questions left to ask you for your book. I have no more questions now, so I am going to repeat the question I asked you in 1975 while I was still ill. This is what I wrote then: 'I have been a chronic severe obsessive for 17 years. As time has gone by I have got more and more obsessions and I have never got rid of any. Lobotomy has been discussed at the hospital but I would die first. Dr. Weekes, can I ever get better?'"

She continued in her 1979 letter, "Remember, that was the original question I asked you in 1975. It seems a long time ago now! As you know, with your help, I have been getting better ever since. I have found that with so many obsessions I have had to work on one at a time, using your method of glimpsing. I know that if one obsession is a strange silly thought, then they all are; but I find in practice I can't flay them all with one swoop. I work on one at a time; get it lukewarm, and then it goes. When they are white hot, if glimpsing is hard I just try to accept.

"I have now got to the stage where I can more or less count those I have left, and they are only a few. They were innumerable. I shall get rid of these, I'm sure of it. But I know I can't do it any quicker than I am. I accept that too.

Hasn't the outlook changed since Dr. T. said I was incurable?"

One of her phobias was fear of getting pregnant. She became pregnant, resisted the suggestion of abortion on medical grounds, and is now the happy mother of a lovely young son.

In September–October 1983 I gave six talks on the BBC and this woman, Anne, was interviewed during these talks. During her last interview she was asked if she was happy. "Oh, yes!" she said in her broad Yorkshire accent, "You have to go through hell to know what heaven is! Oh, yes! I'm happy!"

Thank you, Anne, for coming on television and talking about yourself so openly for the sake of other suffering people. The letters that poured in during and after the talks (12,000 to the BBC apart from those that came to me) told how much people were helped.

**Superpanic: hanging on to a lamppost for support.** "I have superpanics. I feel faint, dizzy, can't breathe properly, and I'm sure I'm going to collapse. I've even hung on to lampposts for support. On top of this, I feel as though I'm 'not there' and that I'm not going to come out of this terrible thing.

"How can I stop this sort of panic from coming on? I do *stay* on the bus, or walk down the street. I've tried to do what you've taught me, but when a panic is as bad as this, how can you expect people to let it come and carry on with what they're doing? Also, I'm drained when I've had an attack; I feel so weak and humiliated, how can I stay calm? I'm sure I'm about to die, and I run for any escape I can see at the time."

This is a striking example of what agoraphobia is all about. Every symptom this woman mentions comes from extreme fear, even terror, and she has put herself into this state because of her fear of the symptoms of fear. She is in a cycle of the symptoms of fear creating more fear.

Unfortunately a very brave woman has got herself into this impasse by thinking she was accepting when she was only putting up with. I appreciate fully how difficult becoming unafraid of panic is while its lash is so scorching. Small wonder so many despair. The lash can be so severe, the spirit seems to collapse beneath it.

While it is possible to take the severest flash without tranquilizers (and many do), I do not expect every sufferer to do so. A rest from practicing with temporary tranquilization can give respite from suffering and help spirits rise until the sufferer is once more ready to face the tiger. After such respite he can let panic flash without crumpling so abjectly before it.

In my practice (I am now retired) I would ask such a person (usually on the telephone) to tell me what she believed I wanted her to do. I insisted that she put her idea of acceptance into her own words until I was sure she knew the difference between it and putting-up-with.

I would ask her to try and *feel* acceptance right in her "middle." When she thought she did, I would say, "Now walk down the street and hope you will panic so that you can practice accepting."

So often a most relieved woman (or man) would return and say, "I did it, doctor!" If she didn't "make it" on that attempt, she usually did on the next. At least, we both persevered until she did.

I stress that there is great difference between temporarily taking tranquilizers for a short respite while in a state of supersensitization and depending on them as a permanent crutch.

Attacks of panic usually decrease in severity and number following a pattern. The person practicing acceptance passes gradually from being terrified and dreading panic to disliking it, then from disliking to finding it no longer mattering. This does not mean that panic no longer comes. It takes time for no-longer-mattering to bring no panic. It is important to realize that panic can still flash and no longer matter. This is the beginning of recovery.

Please, please don't withdraw in terror from the symptoms of terror. There is no way out in withdrawal.

I know that some therapists accompany, or provide

people who will accompany, their agoraphobic patients until they can travel comfortably away from home. However, in my opinion, *these people are left vulnerable to returns of panic.*

I know mine is the hard way to be cured, but if we are to talk of permanent cure, then we must talk of my way. *For permanent cure, a sufferer must learn to cope with his symptoms by learning to become unafraid of them.* He must not be led gently until he gets used to being away from the safety of home. *There is no permanent cure in getting used to being in a certain place so that panic does not come.*

If your heart fails when you read this, and you think that you could never practice what I teach, let it fail as much as it likes, but know that there is nobody who cannot practice this way if he makes up his mind to do it.

**Coping with trembling legs and weakness while talking.** A woman writing about this problem said, "When there's nothing to sit on and I must stand with jelly legs, how do I cope while I stand there shaking?"

The trembling legs and weakness are real. They are not imagined. After an asthmatic has had an injection of adrenaline, his legs tremble too, so that he has to sit, even lie down, for a few minutes. A nervously ill person's trembling and weakness have the same cause. Anxiety releases extra adrenaline. Once more, it's as simple as that.

However, although these trembling legs may seem as if they will give way, they don't. They could even climb steps. They will always support, so why add more anxiety—more adrenaline—by anxiously wondering how much longer they will hold up, how much longer before the fainting comes!

Of course, even when recovered, during occasional stress legs may seem to turn to jelly, but, as I said in *Peace from Nervous Suffering,* jelly legs will always get you there if you let them.

**Change and unreality.** "Why is it that if I visit someone and the decor is changed, or the building has been altered, even slightly (perhaps the inside of a bus has been painted a new color), I immediately panic?"

Change, even slight, can act like a shock. It suddenly makes a nervously ill person aware of the outside world— as if it is demanding attention that he is reluctant to give. Also, if he has been using familiarity as a crutch, new decor could jolt sharply.

These are good experiences and should be welcomed until it no longer matters if the bus seems to be painted violet with yellow stripes!

**The mind goes blank, even when feeling much better.** Even when feeling better a mind can still suddenly seem to go blank. People like this complain that they can't remember the way they're supposed to be going, although they end by going the right way. They say that they feel as if they are in a dream, even when accompanied.

This is only the shadow of introspection—the result of living so much within themselves. It's not important; never be impressed by it. Wait and it will always pass. Of course, it passes more quickly if you don't add second fear.

**Unwanted thoughts.** Never make the mistake of fighting to be rid of unwanted thoughts; relax toward them, let them come, take them with you—but WILLINGLY—and see even the most shocking for what they are: only thoughts.

If you fight to forget unwanted thoughts or try to replace them with others, you make the unwanted thoughts too important, so that forgetting becomes more and more difficult. It is always difficult to forget on command, especially if mentally tired.

A lot of practice at accepting and working while accompanied by upsetting thoughts may be needed to change them into "just thoughts" with no upsetting reaction, holding no fear. Without fear, thoughts that once seemed almost to mesmerize can finally come to matter no longer. No-longer-mattering is the goal, *not* forgetting. One can never be sure of forgetting; memory is a great hoverer. However, if no-longer-mattering has been achieved through understanding and experience, one can depend on it with confidence.

Of course, from time to time, mattering will return. However, when not-mattering has been felt, if only for a moment, the mustard seed of confidence this brings will never actually disappear. As the sufferer pulls himself out of each setback by rediscovering not-mattering, it becomes inbuilt and comes quickly to his rescue whenever a setback threatens. The prize has been won.

**I no longer have to sieve the jelly.** "It sounds ridiculous now, but obsessions are terrifying when you're having them. I can do anything today. I can even make jelly without putting it through a sieve for fear of it containing glass. One of the last things I lost was having to sieve the jelly. That's gone now; I get on with my baking. I've got about eight or nine tins of cakes in the pantry. I'm a good cook and now I can have my friends in and cook for them as they did for me. I want to be able to pay them back because of all the years of hospitality they gave me.

"They were wonderful. They did not understand obsessions, but I said to them, 'Just try and ignore them!' And they did. They didn't say a word. They were super friends.

"You know, I was ill for six years and I couldn't even go into the grocer's shop. I thought they'd have poisonous things on the shelves there—disinfectant and whatnot. I can go now and revel in it. I can walk out too, without checking everything. I can also go into the stationer's and the confectioner's. I haven't faced the pharmacist yet, but I know I'll be able to do that. I'm just wallowing in the relief at going into the other shops. I'll face the pharmacist soon. It's wonderful to be alive now. Thank you."

## Some Bewilderments Cleared Away

**Punishing themselves.** Some nervously ill people complain that they "seem to like punishing" themselves. One added, "That is what nervous illness is all about, isn't it, doctor?"

I have not yet met the nervously ill person who genuinely and deliberately adds to his illness simply to punish himself. His suffering may seem to be self-inflicted because, in his sensitized state, his thoughts, so often fearful, are followed so quickly by distressing symptoms that self-infliction seems the obvious interpretation. Indeed, some therapists believe this, even finding fantastic reasons for it, and they encourage their patients to do the same.

Self-punishment is only apparent, not real. When a nervously ill person says he seems to like punishing himself, he really means, "Judging from my severe and swift reactions to my vaguest anxious thought, it seems as if I'm purposely punishing myself! I can think of no other explanation!" If such a person really liked punishing himself, he wouldn't be asking for help to stop it.

**A tablet before going out?** A woman wrote: "Although I'm making great progress I still need to take a tablet most times before going out. Does it matter?"

There is a big difference between wanting and needing to take a tablet. I suspect that that woman wants to take a tablet because it gives her confidence. She thinks, "I've had my pill so I'll be okay!" Many people, after swallowing a pill, are calm even before it hits their stomach.

That woman should have written, "Although making great progress I still haven't enough courage to go out without taking a tranquilizer." In fairness, I should add that I sometimes prescribe tablets for severely sensitized agoraphobic people to take occasionally before going out. So this woman should ask herself, "Am I severely sensitized and genuinely in need of a tablet to calm me a little, or does taking a tablet simply give me confidence?" If she can answer honestly that the tablet only quiets the symptoms and does not altogether abolish them and that she

49

must still practice accepting and seeing fear through, then she should take a tablet for the time being. If she has to ask herself, "Should I or shouldn't I take a tablet?" the answer is, don't take it. Her need is psychological.

When I sometimes prescribe a tranquilizer for a severely sensitized person, I have first taught them how to go through panic *often enough* without tranquilization so that they know they can do it. With this experience, they understand that they are panic's master and can, while recovering, occasionally soften its blow with a mild tranquilizer—but never with heavy or constant tranquilization.

**How much should I do?** "I'm confused about what I'm going through. I'm accustomed to going to law school and working full-time at night. My health made me take a semester off. I'm wondering if, or when, I can get back into the swing of things?"

One of the hurdles obstructing some people recovering from nervous illness is to decide how much of their fatigue is normal everyday fatigue—the sort they felt before they were ill—and how much is due to lingering illness. In other words, they wonder if they should treat their fatigue with respect "for fear of making it worse" or if they should work on despite it. They are confused.

They need not fear physically overtiring themselves provided they are prepared to accept its effects optimistically. If they work hard one day, they may feel some nervous symptoms more acutely the next, but if they accept this willingly, the symptoms will soon calm. Action and achievement are more important than inaction "for fear of overdoing it." With action accompanied by willing acceptance of any fatigue that may follow, one gradually becomes confident. Working physically, even "overdoing it," will not damage nerves; it's the tension from anxiety that sensitizes and brings fatigue.

This advice also applies to working hard mentally. It's the anxiety accompanying the working that tires, rarely the actual work. The person who has to take a semester off because of the effects of work will be apprensive at the thought of beginning work again. He should understand and expect this and not try to be too stoic. He should let himself be apprehensive and understand that in the circumstances this is to be expected. Fear and lack of confidence will certainly make concentrating and remembering difficult in the beginning; he should expect and understand this. And if he must reread (perhaps many times) a sentence, or a paragraph, before fully understanding it, then he must reread—but *willingly*.

Gradually he will find that studying and remembering will become easier; confidence will return. He will achieve all this by first accepting apprehension, loss of confidence, even muzzy head, and working willingly and quietly determinedly *with them all present*.

**Enjoying life to the full.** "After watching you for several weeks on BBC television I am writing a long overdue letter of gratitude to you. I bought both your books five years ago after hearing about you on the radio. I discovered that I was one of the people who were going to find it extremely difficult to put your teaching into practice, but I persevered, and now from being extremely ill (worse after spending a short time in the hospital) and suffering from agoraphobia and all the accompanying symptoms, I can today enjoy life to the full and live with, and for, my family, who were very supportive through a very trying time. I'm now holding down a job, which seemed an impossibility five years ago. I still have the habit of memory and flashbacks to the old ways, but I practice your method and I always come through. I sometimes think that even today somebody, somewhere, is going to wake up sensitized and be bewildered and not know what to do about it. Your work must never be forgotten and it must go on."

**Waking early; the morning's knife edge.** The upsetting symptoms that can come to a nervous person on waking have been called the startle syndrome. Sensitized nerves can be startled by the slight shock of waking even though the waker may not recognize any shock. Also, the sufferer may go to bed at night feeling relieved and peaceful, only to wake the next morning and feel the same old thumping heart, tingling body, and that old familiar feeling of foreboding. The optimistic feelings of the night before seem to have little influence on the mood of the next morning. The feeling of foreboding may seem so real that the sufferer may search for some impending trouble to explain it. Also, when he first wakes, his nerves may be so "raw" that he feels as if he is balanced on a knife's edge. This is a legacy from the tension of the previous days. Even when the sufferer is almost recovered, some slight renewed stress may bring on again a few mornings of startle and foreboding.

Getting up, going to the bathroom, making a hot drink may be enough to break the spell. At least the sufferer should let the feelings come, not try to push them away. He should relax toward them.

Sometimes, if he continues to lie in a troubled half-sleep, the feeling of being on the knife's edge is accentuated. That half-sleep leaves him vulnerable to little shocks from outside noises, and each shock can "twang" his nerves—hence the knife's edge! It is better to wake right up, move about, perhaps read, than to lie in that perplexed, troubled "raw" state.

**All so quiet in those early hours—so still.** To a nervously ill person who wakes in the very early hours, the quietness can seem threatening; even the sound of the early-morning garbage truck is welcome. At least someone is alive! And, oh, the relief of hearing movement in the house, especially the rattling of cups and saucers!

I once mentioned early-morning quietness to a patient from the country. She laughed and said, "Oh, doctor, you've obviously never lived in the country! You should just hear the animals at our place and the sound of heavy

boots stomping around the kitchen at the crack of dawn!"
Perhaps the sound of heavy boots is comforting someone at
this moment.

Noises that come regularly at a set time—for example, once or twice a week—can be a yardstick to gauge
progress or lack of it. Every Tuesday when the garbage
truck comes, the rattling cans can bring either hope or the
despair of "another bloody Tuesday!"

Sometimes the early-morning waker can be so anxious to return to sleep and blot out those hours of waiting
that she becomes wider and wider awake.

In my opinion there is a stage in nervous illness when
an early-morning sedative may be necessary. It may be
better, if the sufferer is agitated, to shut out those early
hours of lonely suffering than to have him exhaust himself
trying to live through them—accepting one minute, being
overwhelmed the next.

However, waking later—at about five o'clock or after—
is no time for a pill. At this time it's better to wake right
up, listen to the radio, read, or get a hot drink. Taking a
sleeping pill at five or after can make the body feel even
heavier when trying later to heave it off the bed to face
another day.

Some nervously ill people expect to sleep the night
through, irrespective of the time they retire. One woman
said, "I had a bad night last night, doctor!" She'd gone
to bed at seven the previous night, so by three o'clock
she'd already had eight hours of sleep—everybody's
quota. Her problem was that by seven she had to fight
to keep awake. It's so easy for friends to say, "Stay up
late; then you won't wake so early!" This isn't always
true. Eyes that are sleepy early in the evening can pop
open wide as soon as they later hit the pillow; their
owner may then lie agitatedly for hours and end by
taking a sleeping pill after all.

If a severely fatigued person comes to me with a
problem of early waking because of retiring too early, or
because of sleeping during the day, I advise him to sleep

when he feels like it, whatever the hour. As little as one hour's sleep in the afternoon can freshen enough to help get through the rest of the day and does not always interfere with sleeping at night.

It is essential at the stage of severe sensitization to get as much sleep as possible. When a sensitized person is severely fatigued, he needs sleep, not further agitation.

**Driving a car and agoraphobia.** One woman said that in a car she could talk her way through a crisis without anyone seeing her—she could say my words out loud to herself. She admitted that in some ways traveling in a car and perhaps taking a friend was a disadvantage because she came to rely on them both too much. She said, "Should I start again, the right way, alone without the car? I need you personally to tell me, so that I can drum what you say into myself over and over again. Is my car an advantage or is it a disadvantage?"

Driving a car while recovering from agoraphobia is neither an advantage nor a disadvantage; everything depends on attitude, not on the car. Everything depends on whether the agoraphobic uses the car as a prop or not. This woman is using it as a prop. In her heart she knows she must do without props. In her favor, at least she recognizes this. But now she wants to use my words as ejector and prop. I want her to prop *herself* up, doing the things she fears the way I have taught her. She must look for the strength *within herself* to do just that. Strength is always there if we truly want it.

At this stage, she must *not* try to find courage in a command from me! At this stage, after relying so much on car and friend, she must search for her own precious (there is no other word for it) mustard seed of courage and then: Onward! Through!

**Traveling fast in a bus or train.** Allow your body to travel with the moving vehicle. Go with the movement; don't tense against it.

If you stand at a busy street and watch and listen to the heavy traffic go by, it usually seems excessively fast and noisy. However, if you are actually driving a car in that traffic, you are much less aware of speed or noise, because you are going forward with the movement of the car; you are part of the traffic. So, if traveling in a fast bus or train, or any other fast vehicle, take a deep breath, let it out slowly, and let yourself move forward, with the vehicle; don't tense yourself against the movement. Loosen; let go. If you do this, the movement will not seem so fast.

**Just a "touch" of agoraphobia.** In practice I never use the word *agoraphobia*, so my patients have never felt labeled. In my opinion, labeling phases of nervous illness can be dangerous. For example, a woman telephoned today saying she'd had a nervous breakdown for three years and that while that had been difficult enough, one of the doctors at the hospital had labeled her "possibly schizophrenic." She now felt such intense anxiety she didn't know how she could live with it. That careless labeling had presented her with a burden almost too heavy to bear.

Agoraphobia is no more than one aspect of an ordinary anxiety state. A person in an anxiety state may have rapidly beating heart, sweating hands, may feel weak or giddy, and have flashes of panic that grow worse if he is out where he thinks he may be trapped, cannot escape, and so may end by making a fool of himself before other people. Hence, he may avoid going out and mixing with people, especially in a confined situation (public hall, church, and so on).

In my opinion this is the basis of most agoraphobia and is a natural sequence to an anxiety state. And since it is possible to be in a mild or severe anxiety state, it's also possible to have mild or severe agoraphobia. For example, some days a person may feel well enough to go out alone, even to the supermarket, and yet on another day feel unable to face the front door. That is mild agoraphobia. A severe agoraphobic never goes out alone and may even refuse to go if accompanied.

There are certainly grades of the agoraphobic phase of an anxiety state.

**Out of the bog.** Many people trying to recover from nervous illness have the feeling that they must struggle up, up, out of some depth, almost as if they have to drag themselves out of some kind of bog to finally feel *on top* of things—on the same level as life around them. For example, when they hear of a friend going on holiday they think of him as being "on the same level" as the place he is going to—he has only to pack a case and be off! Whereas, for the sufferer, going for a holiday would seem like going to somewhere in the sky above: far, far out of reach.

He does not understand that he feels like this because, to face traveling, he would have to come "out of himself," "up from the depths"; up, out of his gray world of introspection. And it *is* a gray world. The sun may shine, but his mind is so dulled by tiring, endless, anxious introspection, his eye muscles so tensed by anxiety, that the world may actually look gray

Also, to simply be on the same daily level as other people (with no thought of a holiday) seems to require energy he thinks he will never have. The bog is so deep and clinging!

Time, more time, and acceptance make the impossible gradually possible. The bog becomes dry land.

**Can nervous illness cause fits?** "Can a nervously ill person, when in a panic, have a fit? When I was rushed to the hospital with thrombosis in 1950, they said I had had a fit. Actually I had been on barbiturates for many years, five or six a day, and my GP said that my fit was due to the sudden withdrawal of these tablets. You see, I didn't tell the nursing staff that I was taking them. I hope my doctor was right. Even today, I am petrified of the word *fit* and wish people wouldn't use it lightly. Even to write it is making my stomach churn now."

Withdrawal from heavy doses of some tranquilizers, especially barbiturates and benzodiazapines (Valium and its relatives), can cause fits. Nervous illness itself does *not* cause fits. The word *fit* upsets many people, not only the writer of that letter. Understanding clearly what a fit is could help to dispel fear of it. When we look at fear squarely it usually becomes less fearful. Fear doesn't like being looked at! Although this woman now shrinks from the thought of it, I doubt if she has seen a fit. The sooner she learns to face the thought of it without fear, the sooner she will be free to move without fear.

When we want to move our body, our brain sends messages to the muscles concerned. In epilepsy this part of the brain sometimes triggers messages without conscious direction, and the muscles dutifully respond. An epileptic woman is most vulnerable premenstrually, when her brain is irritated by the retention of fluid owing to hormonal imbalance. Regulating fluid and salt intake at that time may be enough to stop the fits.

It's not pleasant to watch someone having a fit, but as usual familiarity brings tolerance. During one of these spontaneous bursts of muscle movement (that's all a fit is), arms and legs flail about. At the same time, the victim loses consciousness and may wet his pants or perhaps bite his tongue. Is that so terrible? Many of us do some of these gymnastic feats at some time. The big difference is that the person in a fit does them all at the same time. Look at it that way.

If you should ever see someone having a fit (after all, Caesar, Saint Paul, Alexander the Great, even Mohammed had them, so why not someone you know?), instead of running away, stay and help. Remove any obstacle that he may hit and so hurt himself.

As mentioned earlier, nervous illness does not cause fits.

**Fear flashes.** "I'm not quite sure what is making me afraid, but I have fear flashes when I look at, or think, certain things; for example, I am afraid I may harm someone. Some days I may just have to look at someone, or touch something, to have that reaction. The picture may seem so clear that it blocks out everything else. This really frightens me."

So many lives have been spoiled by a sensitized body's too acute reaction to some fearful thought. Without such exaggerated reaction, this woman could have reasoned with herself and been able to think, "Of course I wouldn't harm anyone! How silly!" And that would be that. But when thoughts are accompanied by a strong stab of physical fear, the victim may be shocked and bewildered. At such a moment, it is natural to take the thoughts seriously and believe that perhaps he or she really could harm someone and so, perhaps, develop an obsession about it, as this woman has.

If only such people could understand that the thought frightens them only because of their body's sensitized reaction to it and not because it is a real threat. If only they could see the strength of their reaction as part of a physical (sensitized) state, unrelated to truth, and pass through the flash and continue on with the job on hand, how many lives could be saved from exhausting misery! I recently spoke on BBC television, England, about some nervously ill people fearing that they would harm others and received a letter from a woman who, for 30 years, has had this fear. Simply hearing me explain it had freed her. So many years wasted for lack of simple explanation.

**Frightened of being alone.** An American woman wrote, "In the summer I am pretty much okay. I can put the kids on the bike or play with them outside. I can talk with my neighbors, but something awful happens to me come November when I know I will be stuck inside the house for most of the winter.

"My husband takes our only car for the day, and I

haven't driven out of our small town alone since I got sick. I had so many bad attacks in the car that memory of them is holding me back. In your book, you say pull the car over and wait. I've never been able to do that. The longer I sit the worse I get, so I drive quickly in a terrible state—anything to get home.

"When I am in the house this time of year, I feel my illness hovering over my shoulder, and I panic at the thought of it. My children need me; there will be no one to care for them if I weren't here, so I need to be well. I don't know what to do or why I feel like this. My days are lonely and boring. Why am I so dependent on other people? I can do just anything if someone is with me, even drive the car. To sit here a week alone seems impossible.

"Sometimes I feel I am losing my mind because I can't stand my feelings or see a solution. I just know I don't want to be alone."

To bear aloneness contentedly—especially during long, dark, winter days—one has to be very much at peace within oneself. Even those at peace depend on being occupied during the winter. But they have the advantage of being calm enough to sit down and plan for winter days; when the woman who wrote that letter sits and thinks of the long, dark days ahead, she becomes confused by fear and dread. Housework certainly may not hold enough interest, and small children can be demanding and frustrating.

It's important to be able to tolerate being alone; otherwise one can spend a lifetime running away from oneself. Here is an exercise for this woman: when the children are bedded down for their morning naps, she should sit and face the silence, not shrink away from it; she should drench herself in self-awareness. She will find that after a while, her mind will begin to wander. She will think of some job that needs doing; her thoughts will flicker out to the laundry, into the bedroom, or perhaps she will just watch the trees in the garden. She should repeat this exercise whenever she feels overpowered by that moment of aloneness that is so difficult to live through.

When she is prepared to face the quietness in this way, she will find that the hovering monster will gradually stop hovering. She will lose her fear of being alone. It is this, her fear, that brings the undercurrent of tension she dreads.

When she can pass through that moment by facing it and being ready to be swamped by it—not withdrawing from it—she will find she will be able to sit and read a book contentedly, pick up a piece of sewing, and, more important still, be able to plan for the winter days ahead. She will be able to live in the moment, not in fear of it.

**Old age or nervous illness?** "How does one cope with getting old and, at the same time, with the remnants of nervous illness? My illness seems to be taken over by the feelings of advancing age. I'm making no real progress that I can see because of not being able to cope with work or pleasure, or even with a journey by car to go on holiday. And yet I've lived through 15 years of nervous illness! This feeling of great effort takes me back years to the days when I was first going downhill. Perhaps this is why I feel that the cause is now not so much illness as old age?

"With the book [*Hope and Help for Your Nerves*] you have given me, I was able to cope with my illness, and I do lead a reasonable life, but I want to enjoy life to make up for the years wasted. Others live and grow old, but I feel that we phobics gave up living when we became ill, and yet, when we recover, we expect to carry on just where we left off, perhaps years ago. How can I come to terms with all this?

"The things about the house and garden that I used to do, even when I felt bad, I can't get the strength to do now. If I make myself do them I get tired with aches and pains, and it doesn't seem worthwhile. I'm sure there's a link between feeling this way now and the years spent in nervous illness while life was hell. I'm sure I'm feeling the result of this more now because I'm older.

"I'm rambling on about the same thing, but I'm not

alone in this experience; many of my contacts have the same problem. I've been asked, 'Has the fight been worth it?' If I go down again now, I feel I'll never be able to fight back. It has all taken too long. Is it my age that makes me feel unable to cope now, or the memory of my past illness?"

Your tiredness is probably more a legacy of illness than of age, although you don't say how old you are—you talk only of "advancing" years. Naturally resilience and energy decrease with age, and with them go motivation and, so often, interest. Usually the change is gradual, whereas I suspect that you feel old suddenly.

Prolonged nervous illness brings fatigue of the spirit, and, in my opinion, this is probably your main trouble. While you were struggling to recover earlier, it was not so much that you were younger as that you had a goal and hope—two prime motivators. Now you are not only tired by the struggle, you have also lost confidence *because you know you are growing old* and therefore think that feeling tired is irrevocable.

If you have the courage to replace despair with fresh hope and willingness to accept once more, you will gradually feel strength return. Peace of mind is a wonderful healer, and you apparently have little of that now.

Your question has been asked of me many times. I have found that if the questioner stops trying to fathom how much fatigue is the result of nervous illness and how much of old age, and instead does what he can within the limits of his present strength without thrashing himself too severely with doubt and bewilderment, he is surprised how much he can gradually do. Our bodies have great recuperative powers if we remove tension—even in our eighties. I have proved this on myself.

Also, many nervously ill people do not lead active lives during their illness and suffer from lack of exercise—muscles become flabby, and legs tire so easily that sitting or lying, instead of walking, is a constant temptation.

Even the memory of tiredness can bring a feeling of

fatigue, and as for the thought of facing "it all" again . . .!
Small wonder you balk at it.

My advice is: don't look for progress; take each day as it
comes, doing what must be done without asking too many
questions. Don't protest too vehemently; that wastes strength.

Be sure you eat enough nourishing food and are not
taking tranquilizers habitually or too heavy a dose of
sleeping pills at night. As we grow older we tolerate drugs
poorly; small doses can have big effects. Also, if you are
only picking at food, I suggest a moderate dose of vitamins.

Once more, acceptance; but with a fresh heart.

**An on-and-off affair.** "After I first saw you, the level of
my recovery became good enough for me to carry on in an
important job in the public service for 10 more years.
Then I thought: I've handled this well so far, so I can
retire!

"The reason I could manage so well was that although
I sometimes still felt lousy in the mornings and struggled
to work, the moment I became engrossed in work—especially
if it was a research project—I found myself feeling normal.
And then sometimes I had only to become aware of feeling
good when I immediately felt awful again! That's the way
it goes! It's an on-and-off affair, isn't it? Why?"

Finding oneself suddenly well like this can be a
shock, a shock that brings apprehension—and apprehension soon brings a return of nervous symptoms. The
switch from feeling well to suddenly feeling symptoms
again can be so upsetting and bewildering that the nervously ill person can become almost afraid to feel well.
One man said, "I'd rather stay down all the time than go
through this yo-yo business!"

The sufferer must learn to pass through those moments of flash fear and not let them throw him off balance.
On, on, on! Through the flash, through any return of
symptoms; through that pain of contracting heart; through
and on! Recovery always lies AHEAD, however painful the
moment!

**Afraid to feel ordinary feelings.** During recovery, a nervous person may be afraid to feel ordinary feelings. His emotions have been exaggerated for so long that he feels lost, not knowing what to feel. He may think, "Is what I feel now normal? What *is* normal?"

There are so many hazards on the way to recovery. Small wonder acceptance of all strange feelings is the answer. What else could it be?

**Hypochondria.** A nervously fatigued or nervously ill person is suggestible: a pain here, a weakness there, is enough to convince him that he has some strange disease—often multiple sclerosis. Formerly he would have worried little about these symptoms or would have seen his doctor without too much concern.

In my opinion, few nervously ill people are true hypochondriacs. They are simply people who are tired of being ill and are so sensitized that they feel they can't bear the extra strain of worrying about new physical symptoms. They should not be ashamed if they feel they need to visit their doctor frequently to get relief from worry. They should explain to their doctor that in their present state they cannot avoid noticing every new symptom that appears, that their nerves are reacting in an exaggerated way, and that they need the peace they hope his explanation will bring. They are not true hypochondriacs.

**When the airplane doors close.** "What should I do, or not do, when the airplane doors close? I would like to be able to accept an invitation to visit friends in the United States; that is an eight-hour flight. So please could you help me?"

To sit in tension trying not to panic while the airplane doors close could mean trying to sit on panic for the rest of the journey. The anxious traveler should be prepared to panic and think, "Okay, I'm going to panic, so here goes! Let it come!" His very acceptance (real acceptance, not just lip service!) will take the edge off panic. But while he panics he mustn't watch to see if the edge has gone! That's not accepting.

If he does find the courage to take that journey and is willing to panic (the way I teach: loosening the body, letting it slump in the seat, breathing in deeply and out slowly, without withdrawing in panic from panic) he will find that he will gradually become interested in what goes on around him more than in remembering to panic. Actually, the inside of a jet is rather like a busy hotel dining room—so much going on down those aisles.

As I say so often, it's contemplation that is the killer! Anticipating the journey can be worse than making it, but how many have the courage to prove that?

When the frightened person thinks of traveling, he imagines the entire journey being spent in continuous panic. It isn't like that. Once he accepts the closed doors, he may find a certain elation—he has "made it," is actually there, in the seat! He may even talk to his neighbor or watch a movie. Time does pass.

Instead of thinking of seven hours (the journey from London to New York) at a stretch, he should divide the hours into halves and see each half hour through. Also, on a long journey he may feel drowsy and sleep through some of the time. Readers may think, "Not me! I'd never sleep inside an airplane!" They could be surprised.

Some airplane companies have special courses for people afraid of plane travel. They claim to have good results. However, an agoraphobic's fear differs from the usual fear of plane travel. He is not afraid so much of having an accident or the feeling of flying. He is afraid of being hemmed in, unable to escape from his own reactions; afraid of the hell he imagines he could create for himself.

One woman, afraid of panicking in a plane, always carried Valium tablets (just in case). On a particular journey, she managed to see the doors close without having to take a tablet, but when the person beside her started to get worked up, she felt her own panic rising and succumbed to a Valium. Within a few minutes she was calm. It wasn't until that night that she discovered she'd taken a vitamin B tablet, not a Valium. From then on she traveled pill-less.

If you want to travel without the crutch of a tablet, you can. However severe your panic, simply sit back and roll with the punches. Let come what will. Whatever comes won't kill you, and you certainly *won't* have hysterics and go rushing down the aisle as you've been imagining all these weeks. Watch the doors close and let the panic rip; but see it through the right way! That means not withdrawing from it in panic. It means understanding that it is no more than an electrical flash; so see it to the end and don't let an electrical flash stop you seeing your friends in Arkansas! The person who sees panic through is so much more confident, so much more recovered, than the one who sits on panic trying to think of other things to stop panic. Bon voyage!

**The fed-up family.** "I hide your books under the bed now. My family has become allergic to my complaints. They're so fed up with hearing, 'As Dr. Weekes says . . . !' I hope you won't be upset by this, doctor. Your books are a great help to me."

Few people want to hear about another's suffering— especially nervous suffering—and families in particular become gradually browned off. This does not mean that they are necessarily unsympathetic; their own nerves begin to suffer from tension—and living with a nervously ill person means living under tension, especially when spirits rise with the sufferer's improvement and sink with the disappointment of a setback. Few families can survive cheerfully for long, so don't blame your family too much. And yet, to have someone to go to for a little understanding is one of the nervously ill person's dearest wishes. However, as I have said so often, nervous illness can be a lonely business.

**Gratitude.** "To show you how much I have recovered: I went to the hospital this week to a conference on psychiatry and I sat in front of about 50 doctors and answered their questions about my illness. My mouth felt dry and my arms tingled, but I managed to survive this nerve-racking ordeal. In fact, I rather enjoyed educating the audience. Again I say: thank you for making this all possible, doctor."

**Resting on the bed in the daytime.** "I get a lot of help from your books, but I can hardly agree when you say, 'Keep off that bed in the daytime!' I get so very tired doing my level best to carry on with every nerve crying out loudly to rest. Someone rang me just now, and the shock of the telephone nearly killed me. I have suffered all my life with nerves and some of your advice has helped a lot, except that bit about keeping off the bed in the daytime. Oh dear, I thought I could cope with it better. I was going to tell my doctor how much you'd helped me until now! If you could possibly write and explain what you mean by keeping off that bed in the daytime, it would certainly be a help."

This woman is 70 and recently had an accident. Her wounds became infected, and she was in the hospital for weeks and had to return there for further treatment. Of course she should have rested on the bed or couch in the daytime. This is an example of how careful and explicit a doctor should be when speaking or writing. I thought I was careful, but I wasn't thinking of victims of accidents.

Others have been puzzled by my statement about keeping off the bed in the daytime. When I made that statement I was thinking of nervously depressed people who would take to bed as a refuge and lie and brood on their illness, convinced that they hadn't the strength to get up and do anything about it. Also, I thought of the nervously ill person who would lie and worry about his problems and rise later feeling worse than when he lay

66

down. A pillow makes too encouraging a nest for a head full of worry.

Of course people who know they will benefit from daytime rest (as this woman obviously did) should take it. No question.

**Afraid of tall buildings.** Why be alarmed by any strange feeling during nervous illness? Some are bound to come. A baby learning to walk must surely feel strange as he notices how tall the chairs, not to mention his father, seem. However, he goes on and eventually walks, accepting their towering height. That's how we grow up.

A sensitized, nervous person should learn the lesson of accepting strangeness, any strangeness that evokes nervousness, *until it no longer matters*. There will always be tall buildings; they'll never shorten to oblige us; so practice looking at them with acceptance as you breathe in and out deeply and slowly.

Take a brave, especially relaxed look at them as you breathe out. What the heck!

**What causes setbacks?** A setback usually comes in two stages: first, a sufferer's sensitized reaction to some disturbing circumstance or memory, and then his alarm at the return of the old familiar nervous symptoms.

While some sensitization lingers, stress can trigger the return of many, if not all, of the old symptoms. If the sufferer understands and accepts this, they gradually subside. However, if he becomes afraid and tense and thinks, "Here I go again! I'm going to slip right back!" and stays afraid, he opens the door to setback. It's the second fear—the fear of setback itself that he adds—that can entrench him in setback.

A sensitized body can continue to react intensely and swiftly to stress even when the sufferer understands and has reached a stage where the symptoms no longer upset him. Physical recovery so often lags behind understanding and acceptance that it's good to be prepared for an occa-

*easily effected*

67

sional flash of sensitivity; being prepared is the best defense. More time must pass; the way is always on and through, always onward.

With enough practice going into, and out of, setback, setbacks may threaten, even come, but they no longer frighten, and when a setback no longer frightens, it passes very quickly. Indeed, it is no longer a setback—it is not even a halt—it's simply an accepted, even expected, experience on the way to recovery.

**How short is a short illness?** If a sufferer has had no satisfactory treatment for nervous illness, I would call one year of illness short. Illness for a few months would be very short. If a sufferer is having adequate treatment then, in my opinion, three months would be the average time for recovery. I have had patients recover after one interview. Although rare, this has happened.

**How much should I do?** So much depends on the depth of fatigue. A nervously ill person may feel so exhausted when he finally decides to get off the bed and face recovery that he may need physical support—an arm to lean on. However, with determination and the right kind of effort, nervous fatigue can pass surprisingly quickly—within three or four weeks. Having some kind of occupation, fortified by acceptance, restores strength faster than resting on the couch.

Also, a nervously ill person who, on rising, feels that he hasn't the strength even to make the bed will often find that by the end of the day's work he has more energy than when he first got up. Physical work exhausts less than does anxious introspection.

Don't worry about how much you should do; simply go and do what has to be done, willingly. Rest at intervals, again willingly, and do not feel anxiously guilty about "all that work piling up."

Never push yourself to prove how much you can do; pushing means tension. On the other hand, don't go around the house working at a snail's pace for fear of pushing. It really doesn't matter whether you work quickly or slowly, as long as you work with willing acceptance of how you feel and of how much you have left undone.

**Strenuous sport while depleted?** A man asked this question.

I have yet to meet the depleted person who wants to play strenuous sports. However, I have seen some young people who thought they were too weak to leave the beds on which they had been lying for years play tennis after only a few weeks of the right treatment.

One man, more or less confined to bed for nine years, said he felt so ill he hadn't the strength to read my book *Hope and Help for Your Nerves;* a friend read it to him. And yet, after listening to these readings and then practicing walking with golf clubs as crutches, he was playing tennis within six weeks. His story was published in the *New York Times Magazine* around Christmas 1977. One finds strength quicker when active than when lying on the couch waiting for it to come.

I encourage patients to be active, but before I would advise strenuous sport I would need to examine the adventurer. Swimming I advise because it need not be strenuous and if in salt water is especially soothing to those trying to come off tranquilizers. It brings its own sedation.

Also, during the agitation that can accompany drug withdrawal, exercises help "let off steam," and I recommend them.

**Our power to adapt.** A woman recovering from nervous illness went to stay with some friends at the seaside. When she first saw the cottage her heart sank. It was weatherboard and old and reminded her of similar cottages in which she had lived years ago when young and poor. The memory was depressing, and she was further depressed when she remembered she was committed to stay for a month!

However, she let the first shock pass and found, after a few days, that she quite enjoyed resting on the sunny veranda and that the store on the corner was handy; the woman next door was kind; and the linoleum on the floor and the ugly old-fashioned dresser in the kitchen no longer bothered her. The disliked kitchen became a warm, welcoming place.

We should always remember to let the first shock pass and never run away too soon. Our power to adapt is irrepressible if we give it a chance.

**When is a person "too old" for recovery?** Much depends on circumstances, and unfortunately, when a person is old, these may not be very encouraging. An old person may feel himself a burden to family and friends—to those friends left! Having to put on an act before the family accentuates loneliness, weariness, even apathy. It's sometimes difficult to decide how much weariness and depression are due to circumstances and how much to old age. One man, always tired, always lying down, was found to be diabetic; with treatment he now spends hours in the garden. He said, "I could never work out what was natural tiredness for my age and what was an underlying illness!"

Many people in their seventies have this same puzzle. I am so often asked, "Is it my nerves or just my age, doctor?" An old person should be examined regularly by a caring doctor. Age itself is no bar to recovery from "nerves." So much of the trauma in growing old is psychological. One has but to see the effect of turning 70 on some people to understand the power of suggestion. A friend said to me, "I was all right when I was 69. The minute I turned 70 I felt old!" If we could grow old like other animals without knowing our age, there would be many more healthier and fewer depressed old people.

Of course, recovery is helped by finding an interesting occupation, particularly in the company of other people. Finding an interesting occupation is the biggest stumbling block to recovery for young people; for old people it's like searching for the crock of gold at the end of the rainbow. It is so easy to prescribe, so hard to find.

A friend told me about her father, aged 92, for whom they were trying to find some new occupation. They made one offer and he said, "I don't want to do that! I want something with some future to it!"

And how's this for spirit? A woman wrote, "I'm extraordinarily better and count myself cured. I'm 89 and have to wear a hearing aid. Most people have to wear theirs during the day, but I have to wear mine at night as well. I feel I must hear the clock ticking. I panic if I can't, so I have two clocks to be on the safe side. Also I can't sleep in the dark without a night-light.

"When I think of the hours and days I walked about the streets because I couldn't stay in the house, it seems a small thing to ask. I owe everything to your kind help. My lip-reading teacher had a sudden attack from working too hard. She is having a year off. I lent her your book, and she has found it a great help and is much better."

So here's a woman of nearly 90 asking about complete cure. that should cheer on the babes of 70. But what is there for her to be "really cured of"? A ticking clock and a little night-light. Surely she is entitled to both.

When old, it's so easy to be apprehensive at night. During the day, with familiar homely things around, apprehension dims but in the dark aloneness at night, the ticking clock and the little light mean that home is still there even in the dark.

**Agoraphobia and living in a city like New York.** "I developed agoraphobia about 10 years ago when New York started to deteriorate so badly. I don't travel in the subway or walk around at night for fear of being mugged. I really feel this should be included in any talk about agoraphobia.

"Of course books and articles are now being written about agoraphobia; in fact, it is the 'in' thing. I don't find that very funny. To me the reality is too painful. Agoraphobia should not be a cocktail or TV session curiosity, should it?"

To be afraid of moving around in a big city after dark or of traveling in the subway because of legitimate fears of being mugged is not agoraphobia. While a person can circulate freely when in an area safe from mugging, can go on holiday, attend meetings, and so on, he is not agoraphobic. In a smaller, safer town he would probably travel everywhere without fear.

It is true that there is much talk about agoraphobia today. Before the early sixties few had heard of it, and later, when they did, the idea of a man or woman (usually woman) staying at home for years for fear of traveling away from home—even being afraid to go to the mailbox to post a letter—intrigued so many people that it soon became a conversation piece and a media pet. Better to have people interested and even gossiping about agoraphobia than being ignorant of its existence.

Some of the amused people were not so flippant when they suddenly discovered the cause of Aunt Ethel's persistent refusal to go on a holiday with them, or a friend's persistent refusal to dine at a certain restaurant. These are real examples. After being on television or radio, I sometimes found a member of the staff waiting for me at the studio exit. They would confide secretly about some member of their family or friend who, they now discovered, was agoraphobic.

In one city, the driver of my car invariably came with me while I broadcast and stood in the shadows in the studio. I said, "Bill, you don't have to accompany me while I talk!" He answered, 'Oh, yes I do, doctor! I understand now what's been wrong with my wife these last three years and I'm learning how to help her. She's listening in too!"

Better small talk than no talk.

**An original cause.** If, by finding an original cause, a nervously ill person loses his fear, then he can be cured, because losing fear is simply another way of describing recovery. However, cure only occasionally lies in finding an original cause, because, even with the cause found, nervous symptoms so often remain. Sensitization has the last word, and finding an original cause does not necessarily desensitize. The sufferer may have become afraid of physical nervous symptoms.

In my opinion, in the past there has been too much emphasis on curing by finding possible subconscious causes; thankfully, today therapists are more willing to admit that an original cause may no longer be working, may even be unimportant, at the time when the patient comes for help. Great relief to us all!

**That niggling feeling: could the symptoms return?** A man wrote, "Although I feel I'm almost cured, will I always have that niggling fear that all the symptoms could come back?"

The niggling fear will linger so long as the thought of a return of symptoms brings apprehension. When a sufferer is close to his past suffering, memory can bring a very vivid picture of those upsetting experiences. Small wonder that memory becomes accompanied by apprehension and a nagging dread that "it" may return.

The writer said that he is almost cured. To be so near cure he has surely learned how to accept and so quiet some nervous symptoms. He can do this again. He should encourage himself with that thought, and instead of staying tensely on guard, trying to keep setback at bay, he should face the niggling fear and be prepared to let the symptoms come, full blast if necessary. If he does this, the niggling fear will gradually subside. The subsidence is quicker if he has an opportunity, not once but several times (even more than several), to pass through the return of symptoms successfully. Always, no-longer-mattering holds the key that brings future peace with no more niggling fear.

I said "no more niggling fear." However, the truth is that even when the return of symptoms no longer matters, carrying niggling fear can become a habit and can persist for some time. Once again, acceptance and letting time pass are joint healers.

**That persistent inner voice.** There is a persistent inner voice that challenges the nervous person to think the worst, a little voice that says, "Others can do it, others can recover, but not you!" A nervously ill person's mind can play strange tricks, and he is too easily impressed by them. He doesn't understand that it is natural for an inner voice to complain as his does, while he is still so sensitized.

Recovery often follows similar patterns, and one of these is the frequent development of a negative inner voice. Obstructive thoughts are normal, very human, in the circumstances. Their voice should be heard. Let it have its way; it will take it, anyhow. Let it say what it wants to; let it bring plenty of fear, but *watch it doing it;* while you have the courage to watch without letting it overpower you, you will gradually feel yourself becoming detached from its babbling.

**Fainting.** Very few nervously ill people faint. From time to time, many "feel faint," but few actually faint. This is because the faintness a nervously ill person experiences is often self-induced, and most sufferers, when they start to work themselves up for fear they will faint, usually manage to divert their attention from the fainting to finding an escape route. They are so used to defeating their feeling of faintness by flight that they always sit near a door, so that they can depart quickly if necessary.

But why do they feel faint in the first place? I'm not talking about the person who has been only "picking at" his food and is possibly undernourished or anemic. I speak of a nervously ill but adequately fed person. Such a person feels faint because he, in any feared situation, continuously gives himself little shocks by suggesting, "What if I have to sit near the front? . . . How much longer will I be able to sit through this? . . . Will that man *never* stop talking? . . . What if I do faint? . . . I can feel it coming! . . . What if I can't get out, and faint?" Shock after shock. Most people's nerves can stand this onslaught for a long time, and the victim may feel only lightheaded. As I said, the nervously ill person rarely faints.

The lesson to be learned is that no nervously ill person need faint if he or she is prepared to do as I'm constantly advising—and that is, not to add second fear. If you are in the situation where you fear fainting, let your body go loose (relax) to the best of your ability and be prepared to accept whatever feelings it brings without adding the extra shock of "Oh my goodness, what's going to happen now?"

It is strange how we keep our grip on ourselves by being prepared to release it. We never keep the right kind of grip by holding tensely on to ourselves, as so many wrongly believe. By abandoning ourselves to whatever our body may care to do, we release the tension that is fatiguing the nerves controlling our blood vessels, and they are able to contract normally and prevent blood from pooling in our legs; we also relieve the stress that may sometimes activate the vagus nerve to slow the heart's beating. After a while we do not even feel faint.

So much of a nervously ill person's suffering is self-induced through ignorance and bewilderment. It is also induced by what he thinks is the hovering shadow of having someday, somehow, to face the ultimate. No one is quite sure what he means by this, but each is convinced that it is something terrible. The ULTIMATE—in other words, the worst that could possibly happen—is no more than a creation of fear and imagination working together, a bogeyman that will disappear if the sufferer has the courage to say "Boo!"

Some people do faint more readily than others, whether they are nervously ill or not—for example, soldiers on parade, who stand for hours in the same place. This kind of faintness can be corrected by moving one's body as much as the situation permits.

Please don't think, after reading this, that if you have to stand still anywhere you must immediately begin to fidget. As it is, the nervously ill person who stands quite still for any length of time would be hard to find. Remember, no nervous person need faint because of his "nerves" if he lets his body loosen and accepts whatever feelings it brings him, even the sensation of "feeling faint."

**Fear of dying.** I could tell you that "what can't be cured must be endured," and so it must, but how to endure a fear of death that may haunt for years—sometimes a lifetime—while yet being prepared to face death when it actually comes? That is the point.

Sudden death gives no time for its contemplation, so why should we fear it? It seems foolish to worry about something we would know nothing about, and yet so many are afraid of sudden death. Many nervously ill people fear that, at the peak of their panic, they may collapse and die. They read about people who do die in a moment of extreme emotional stress, and they see themselves doing the same.

During my experience as a doctor treating hundreds of nervously ill people, I have not known one to die during a panic spell. I suspect that the people we have read about who died this way already had a "heart condition" and that the extra stress was the last straw. Nervously ill people have, as a rule, experienced so much panic that their heart has already shown them, again and again, how much it can endure; indeed, they often have very strong hearts. Trust your powers of adaptation. They will not fail you as readily as you may imagine.

While some people are concerned with sudden death, most are concerned with death that may come gradually, when they are old. Here again, I speak as a doctor. I have rarely attended a person actually dying who realized that he or she was dying. A few do, but very few. Nature blunts the edge of her sword; even during the years before our death nature helps us; our habits and our demands on life change. At 20, the weekend means activity—dinner and dance and tennis; at 70, we'd rather sit by the fire and read. Activity naturally slows down. If we are prepared to go along with nature as willingly as possible, she will make our death rather like our birth—while we will be the star performer, we will be unaware of the performance.

I don't say that there may not be suffering for many during those last months—even years—but here again, age dulls feeling to a certain extent; inevitability brings its own anesthesia.

Creatures of adaptation that we are, we adapt even to the thought of death. Let me tell you about one old man. He needed an operation on his throat. The surgeon explained that if he had the operation his life could be prolonged by as much as three or four years. The man asked, "How long will I live if I don't have the operation?"

The surgeon replied, "About six months."

"Then," said the patient, "I'll settle for six months, thank you. If I go into hospital I'll lose my lodgings, and they're very hard to find these days!"

I remember looking at the man in amazement. The surgeon, elderly himself, showed no surprise. He turned and said to us, his group of students, "The philosophy of old age!" Understanding this was beyond me. Today, I understand it well.

Youth and middle age are for active living, and we should not rob it of any of its joy by dreading something that, when it comes, we may actually welcome, or at least may be unaware of. I remember a woman of 80 who had feared the thought of dying all her life. When the time came she said to me, "I don't mind dying I've seen everything and I've been everywhere and I'm very tired. Elsie's gone. Fred's gone. Funny, isn't it, I feel more a part of them than I do of the people here. There's not much pleasure left now. What a silly I've been all these years worrying about dying. Now I want to go!" It is so often like that.

Another woman of 84 saw her grandchild, aged four,

for the first time. She said, "This has made living through the last few years worthwhile!" And yet to outsiders, including her family, she'd seemed happy enough during those last years. So when she did die her daughter always had the comforting thought, "Mother didn't mind going, really!"

Have you ever thought that going through a surgical operation must be very like dying? As we're given the injection, we are asked to count; by the time we reach number seven, we're back in bed, with a nurse bending over us asking us if we feel all right? And yet three or four hours may have passed between "seven" and the vision of the nurse. What happened to us during that time? Nothing we know about. Did those four hours worry us? No, they were as nothing. Surely death is not so very different? If you are religious and believe in life after death you have inbuilt comfort; if you have no such belief, remember that operation and comfort yourself with the thought, "Why be afraid of something I will know nothing about?"

Therefore, however old you may be, live each day as it comes and always plan for the future. If, when you are 90, you need a new tea set, buy it. Don't think, "I won't buy that. It's too late!" If you have only a little time to enjoy, enjoy it with what time you have, and enjoy it right up to the very last minute. The days that come when you aren't there won't worry you, because you won't be there to be worried!

Concern yourself only with the days you are alive, and enjoy them to their fullest. Leave the rest to nature, or to God, as you prefer, and never be bluffed into fearing death, however you imagine it may come.

**The first panic.** "The first time I panicked was out shopping in Exeter. I'd had a cup of tea in the store and had gone up to the powder room. I felt so panicky I asked to be taken home. That experience so upset me that I didn't go to Exeter for ages.

"I panicked again three weeks later. I was tense at the

time, having been to the dentist a few days earlier; a set appointment always worries me. Just two days later came my granddaughter's christening. It was a lovely service in a delightful church and I enjoyed it very much. There was a buffet meal afterward at a local hotel. I enjoyed watching the people looking after my mother (she was 85) and helping my 18-month-old granddaughter with her meal. I got chocolate on my hands and decided to wash them.

"I know the hotel well, but the powder room is newly built and strange. It was empty when I got there. I can see now the connection between the panic in Exeter and the panic on this occasion. The trouble started when I locked the toilet door. I always find locking doors threatening. First comes the fear, and everything seems to recede. I know what I am and what I am doing, but I seem to be in a dream, to have lost my identity. I remember at Exeter wondering if I was still alive. In the middle of all this, I remembered Dr. Weekes saying, 'Take no notice of strange feelings. Loosen and accept!'

"I washed my hands, and they took ages to dry under the dryer. I looked in the mirror. I felt awful and I looked awful, and thought, 'I'll do my hair and powder my nose and then go back.' This I did. I then went back along the corridor to the dining room, sat down, and carried on where I had left off. The feeling of panic had almost subsided.

"The next day I was very tired, but I decided that I would not be put out by it this time although I kept remembering it.

"Doctor, had the feeling reached its peak, or could it have got worse? Was it likely to have lasted any longer? If that was 'it,' I know I can cope with it again should it recur."

To wish for reassurance that "it" could grow no greater shows that this woman still fears panic, and while she is afraid she harbors the seeds of further panic. For her, "it" certainly could have got worse had she not coped the way she did. She must try not to rest secure in the feeling "I can stand *that* much!" She must know that *she can face and go through panic however fiercely it may come*. She can have this comfort: even the fiercest flash has its limit! Only when she can pass through any flash the right way will she lose fear of both "it" and the menacing shadow of "perhaps."

Panic takes many strange forms, and "recession" is one of them. I talk about this in my book *Peace from Nervous Suffering* and have already mentioned it in this book. Recession is a feeling of thoughts going back, back, right to the very back of the head; it is frightening, because the sufferer wonders if he will ever come back to be himself again. Recession is no more than tension's screws clamping more tightly than usual—a feeling of being encased in one's own mind—identity lost! It is essential to recognize and not be bluffed by tension's strange tricks. The calmness that comes with the relaxation (even the slightest) that understanding brings (it came to this woman to some extent when she remembered my words and returned to her friends) helps to unclamp the clamp. There is nothing to fear.

This woman's next question was about going to Tavistock even though feeling unwell. She said, "I now think I can cope with panic on traveling, but when I'm not well I can't decide whether it's just an excuse or should I make myself go?"

"Not well" is a vague expression. If she had influenza with a temperature, she certainly should not go—moderation in all things. However, while she wonders if she is making an excuse, she can't be very ill. So, if there is good reason to be at Tavistock, she should go—doubts and all.

If she decides not to go, accepting this negative decision (unless the thermometer says: stay!) will be very difficult. Most nervously ill people find accepting negative decisions difficult, especially if there is a shadow of doubt. For example, this woman would think, "Perhaps I should have gone! Perhaps I'm being cowardly!"

True acceptance means accepting a negative decision once it is made. Swinging from "Perhaps I should have!" to

"Per<u>haps I shouldn't!" is tiring and co</u>
<u>nothing for confidence</u>. Going to Tavistoc
obligation there despite feeling "lousy" is a g
dence booster. In my first book, I say, "Wait on no
The mood waiter waits one heck of a long time!

So, off to Tavistock!

# 4

# Journals to Patients 1975–82

During 1968–70 I sent quarterly journals of encouragement to approximately 1,300 nervously ill people (mainly in the United Kingdom) who were using my book *Hope and Help for Your Nerves* and my recordings for recovery. These journals were published in my second book, *Peace from Nervous Suffering*.

In 1971 I made a survey of approximately 500 of these people, which was published in the *British Medical Journal*, May 26, 1973.

During 1972–74 I continued sending quarterly journals, which I condensed into a composite journal and published in my book, *Simple, Effective Treatment of Agoraphobia*.

During 1975–82 I sent one journal yearly—quarterly journals were no longer needed, because so many people were recovering. These journals are published here.

A casual reader may query the repetition in these journals; however, the nervously fatigued or nervously ill person will recognize repetition as treatment. He wants the advice stressed until he *feels* it, not only reads it. He needs the motivation feeling brings; repetition emphasizes and so encourages feeling.

The following journals were sent to approximately 2,000 nervously ill people, mainly agoraphobic, in the

United Kingdom, the United States, Canada, Australia, and Africa during 1975-82.

# WILLINGLY—*May 1975*

Once more I write to you from Australia. Sometimes I must leave England or the United States to return to my family out here. However, I think of you and often wonder about your progress. I have said so much in books, tapes, and journals that it will be difficult for you not to know, almost by heart, what I want you to do and how to do it. And yet there may be many of you who still need encouragement and guidance.

It is possible to reduce all my messages to a few simple words. Actually, my teaching can be reduced to one word. If you asked me what, of all I have taught you, you should remember, I would say: remember to try to always act WILLINGLY. Willingly face the day, willingly take what comes, and especially willingly (as willingly as you can manage, to begin with) accept the symptoms you dislike so much. Remember that word willingly, willingly, WILLINGLY. However, don't try to let *willingly* work for you until you have been assured by your doctor that your symptoms are caused by "nerves."

Although I have talked to you about almost every aspect of your nervous illness, I have not yet discussed those years "lost" in illness. During your illness you have naturally concentrated so much on yourself that you have not fully lived in the outside world (that is putting it mildly for some of you) so that those years seem lost; as if there is a no-man's-land between you—as you are now—and that earlier, well you.

Actually, you've learned a great deal during those apparently lost years. You've learned to be compassionate, how to understand and possibly help others, and how to appreciate simple things. It may seem as if your normal life came to an abrupt end when you first became ill and that there is an unbridgeable gap between then and now. It seems unbridgeable because you are looking back and are trying to build a bridge *behind* you to link up with today. The bridge can be built only by going quietly forward until the feeling of normality, which recovery gradually brings, builds it. Then you find yourself automatically linking up with the old you.

I appreciate that some of you are still battling and haven't made the progress you think you should have made. This is most probably because you haven't practiced the way I've taught you, or the conditions in which you are trying to recover have been especially discouraging, or you may have been physically ill. I know some of you have been physically ill and have carried on in spite of this. This is true courage.

If you carry out my teaching the right way in spite of failures in the past, you will recover; so, however disappointed or discouraged you may be, start practicing again WILLINGLY. I especially want to encourage those who have done well, who even thought they were over the final hurdle, perhaps even recovered, and who in spite of this are now in a setback. This can be almost devastatingly disappointing. However, nothing you have learned has been lost, so don't whip yourself because you think you have slipped from the right path after so much success, and don't exhaust yourself wondering how it could have happened to you! You may even be the mainstay of a special group of nervously ill people and view your setback as a special calamity. Actually it will help you revise your knowledge of nervous suffering and of how to come out of it. It may even help you to be more patient with those others who seem stuck in a rut in their illness. Being obliged to come through setback yet again may even humble you, and we're all better for a touch of humbling now and then.

So I want to encourage those discouraged to start once more. I think of you struggling away in those far lands. You are such brave people. Don't drop out of the recovery race, however many your past failures may be. Failure counts only if you let it.

## DEFUSING THE BOMB—*January 1976*

It hardly seems fair that I should be talking to you in bright sunshine while so many of you are in the cold and rain. However, you did have a good summer last year, didn't you?

In this letter I will talk about *defusing the bomb*.

Some nervously ill people think they are accepting by "learning to live with" their illness. (Even some doctors say, "You'll have to learn to live with this!") That is, some people are prepared to compromise and live with some aspect of their illness without making an effort to rid themselves permanently of all of it. They are resigned to some defeat. This is not the *right* kind of acceptance. I want you to learn how to cope with your illness until you are free of all of it—no compromise. I don't want those who are agoraphobic to resign themselves permanently to not go here, not go there, not travel in this or that.

The acceptance I teach means going forward, doing the things dreaded, and doing them with utter acceptance of whatever nervous symptoms, sensations, or experiences may come while doing them. It means accepting even revulsion against the thought of doing and still doing: but DOING the right way (you remember?—the deep breath, the letting go, and the marching forward). Yesterday I showed a woman how she was agitating herself by withdrawing from the thought of the situation she feared. For her it was flying from Sydney to Melbourne two days later, and she hardly knew how she would live through those two days.

I explained it was as if she had a lemon in her tummy that she squeezed every time she thought of that menacing journey, and that the more she squeezed the more agitated she became because the more stress hormone she produced. I said, "Take your hand off that lemon. Don't keep squeezing it!" She had already learned how to cope with panic after 40 years of misery but did not appreciate that she should cope with agitation the same way. It was the feeling of agitation, of restlessness, that upset her now.

I taught her to go forward into the agitation; to let herself *be agitated;* to stop withdrawing in apprehension from it, to even try relaxing toward it. In other words, to stop continually squeezing that lemon.

She managed the journey home and telephoned today. She said that what helped her most was the thought, "Hands off that lemon!"

If you are like this, when you go forward into your fears, even into agitation, you gradually DEFUSE THE BOMB. Every time you come out of setback, you have defused it a little more; every time you practice the right way, you defuse it still further. Someday, when you do something daring, like visiting a distant town or riding on your own in a bus or train, you will find that even though you expect to panic, *panic does not come*. Your practice at acceptance has finally taken the power out of panic, the fuse out of the bomb. This doesn't mean that you will never panic again. Far from it. That old demon will certainly appear again; but once the bomb has been defused, panic loses its power to bluff you. There may be short bursts (even a long one!), but you are able to pass through these with understanding and confidence.

Also, instead of being overwhelmed and discouraged by setback, I want you to understand that to be able to be in a setback means that you must have previously made progress. Be glad of that and accept the setback as part of recovery and quietly go on. As I said, every time you come through setback you defuse the bomb still further. It all adds up, so don't waste a good setback lamenting about it. Use it for further defusing. Make the most of it.

I have mentioned the strange tricks that fatigue can play. There is that strange ability to do things well one day, and yet, the next day, be unable to even contemplate doing them. We make the mistake of judging ourselves while we are fatigued, without recognizing our incompetence as fatigue.

I'm still impressed by the fatigued nervously ill person's inability to quickly change a point of view. On the other hand, I am intrigued by his ability to do this if he approaches the change gradually, with quiet but relaxed determination. *Gradually* is the keyword. All comes gradually. Set your goal and float toward it. You can't strenuously argue yourself better. If you try, you will not stop arguing. Getting better is a job for time and continued acceptance (or repeated trial at acceptance!).

Fatigue also underlies much depression, especially the fatigue of repeatedly doing uninteresting things. But even here, if work is done willingly and spirits are not being continually drained, a natural resilience helps to carry one above mundane tasks. By willingly I mean to even willingly carry the "heart of lead," the "horse's hoof" in the tummy, to work with this aching heaviness and not try agitatedly to find something to do to distract and help lose it. To go forward in depression with willing acceptance will work a miracle. This teaching is based on physiological laws that have always worked and always will. Trust them.

For those of you who have worked and progressed well, my thanks and congratulations. For those still struggling, don't lose heart. Have some more shots at defusing the bomb. But make sure you understand clearly what I have taught you.

## THE FRONT LINE OF BATTLE—*July 1976*

When I heard that the temperature in Britain was 90°, I wished I had taught you more about the similarity between some of the symptoms of nervous illness and those felt during very hot weather: those flushes that seem almost like mini-panics, the pounding heart, the feeling of fullness in the face, the sweating, fatigue, and so on.

So don't be discouraged during the heat by any symptoms resembling nervous symptoms: always remember that these are the usual symptoms that can come with stress, and a very hot day can be stressful; so please don't be tricked into thinking that they mean the return of your illness.

Some of you want so badly to lose your symptoms that you keep yourselves in an almost constant state of anxiety about it, and because of the stress anxiety brings, the symptoms persist. Can you understand this? You are like a dog with a can tied to its tail. Round and round he goes, trying to get rid of it. You go round in a cycle, *anxiously* trying to be rid of the symptoms of anxiety that of course then chase you!

So I want to give a special prescription to those who are tired of revolving in that cycle. First: try to be less anxious about the symptoms. If you can manage only a little less anxiety, there will be less stress, and the symptoms, because of this, must calm a little. Second: play my cassettes as often as you can manage. Make this effort. Some of the cassettes are long, so don't necessarily play the entire cassette at one sitting. Now—and here comes the important part of this prescription—at this stage you need only listen. You need not even try to go out and practice what I teach you. JUST LISTEN, but again and again.

After you have spent a week or more listening, you will absorb more of my teaching than you realize, and one day, when out, if you have one of your crippling "spells," you will find that you have an inbuilt little voice that supports and tells you what to do. What is more, you will find yourself automatically doing it. So, those of you who are tired and discouraged and feel like giving up, GIVE UP, but play the cassettes and listen. You will be surprised at the result.

This morning a woman reminded me of an aspect of recovery from nervous illness that I can never emphasize too much. It is the strangeness, especially during the early stages. This woman, who had been complaining of feeling unreal, said that during the previous weekend, as soon as she started practicing its acceptance, the feeling of unreality had come more vividly than ever, and more often than before. She was now confused and worried, because she was sure she had done everything I had advised. She said she had accepted the feeling, had not tried to puzzle out what it meant, and not even tried to get rid of it or run away from it. She had even been prepared to work with it there. Yet it stayed. She couldn't understand this.

This woman had not done *everything* that I had advised her. She had forgotten that I had warned her in my books that this very experience could occur and that it is what deters so many people from trying to recover on their own without any outside help. As soon as they begin to question whether they are working the right way or not, they fall into the trap of being at first bewildered and then despairing. They feel bereft; they think even my teaching has failed them: there is no hand to grasp.

I reminded her that in my book I wrote that in the beginning, when a sufferer first practices what I teach, he is deliberately putting himself in the front line of battle, putting his head on the block. It has to be like this, because instead of pushing a disliked feeling aside (and this sometimes works for a while), he faces it, may even go looking for it. Being ready to practice coping with what is feared often means concentrating on it. This woman's decision to try to cope with the feeling of unreality that weekend so alerted her to it that it became a highlight of the weekend.

Although she was comforted by this explanation, I expected her to have a grueling week; however, if she continued as I had taught her—with willing acceptance of the feeling—it would gradually become less and less important until it would hardly ruffle her.

Everything comes back to willing acceptance. Sometimes I write the words *Willing acceptance* on a prescription form for a patient. Some print it in large letters on a card, which they hang in a prominent place in their home—usually over the kitchen sink.

Will you try once more to do as I teach you? Even if you only play the cassettes and listen. I send you all my encouragement.

## A MIRACLE FROM WITHIN—*October 1977*

If only I could gather you all together and really drive the message home that recovery lies in your understanding of acceptance and practicing it and not in expecting an outside miracle. I did speak to some of you in London this year, and to others in Liverpool.

Recently I helped a woman through a period of nervous "exhaustion" when she thought she'd reached the end of her tether and couldn't go one step further. She had been doing very well and had even held down a job, but now she was at the stage where she could hardly find the energy to take the car out of the garage to take her little girl to school. Earlier in the month she had had a "queer turn" while out, and this is why she had worked herself up into a proper state about driving into town. She was at the stage of thinking, "I'll never go near that place again!"

So we started off from taws—exhaustion, panic, influenza, family illness, and complete (or so she thought) lack of confidence, with added unwillingness to go on with the struggle. But gradually, with encouragement to go out while she was so "done," she came to see that she could still function even in those "terrible" moments. By working at those times, she gradually built a little platform of confidence from which to go into town, drive her daughter to school, and even visit a sick relative at the hospital.

On one occasion I spoke harshly to her. I have rarely done this to any patient. I was so exasperated, because I had spoken to her so often, and she knew so well what she had to do to recover but was making no effort. I wanted to shake her out of herself, and I succeeded. Although she is

90

still very, very tired and upset by a recent death in the family and has *another* cold, she says she knows she's on the right road again. She has glimpsed recovery once more, because she no longer balks at doing things when she "doesn't feel like it." She no longer waits until she feels better. She has found the eye of the hurricane.

Sailors say that in the middle of a hurricane there is a place of peace, which they call the eye. To find it the ship must first pass through the storm. This woman had faced and passed through while the storm raged, and although her symptoms did not disappear, she felt the peace of achievement and the beginning of being freed from her chains. She understood that with the new inner peace she now had, the symptoms would gradually calm.

This letter is to encourage you to find the eye of your hurricane; so, onward little ship into the storm, into the eye of the hurricane, but willingly with acceptance.

## CLEARING AWAY THE MISTS—*October 1978*

Gauging the stage of your progress is difficult, so please forgive me if the following talk does not apply to you. However, there is surely some help in it for everyone. I am writing this in London. We are having an Indian summer, and I'm not making the most of it because I've joined the band of the many who trip on a London pavement. I've sprained my foot. What a waste of such lovely weather!

In a letter recently, a woman wrote, "Nobody can convince me that I won't go berserk, collapse, if I find myself in a situation I can't handle and when I'm a long way from home. How could I cope if I felt I couldn't stand another minute of it and there was no way to escape? Perhaps you could elaborate on this in some future article."

In other words, she longs for some cure outside herself that will rid her of her fear. She hasn't accepted yet that riddance must come from her. It would help her if she could see clearly just what would happen if she found herself in such a situation; now she sees it as if through a haze. Two factors are to be considered here. First, how can she stop the intensity of her panic from building up, and second, if she can't, what will happen then? She must understand that only she encourages her glands to keep secreting the chemicals that increase panic. I'm not talking about that flash, that lightning flash, of first fear that seems to come automatically to a sensitized person in a frightening, or even only slightly frightening, situation; for example, a mere cold blast of wind! No one, let alone a sensitized person, can immediately control that flash, and I never ask them to. But this first, apparent, automatic flash, comes as one single flash. And always passes. *The panic that continues flashing must be added by the sufferer himself to that first flash.* And it is so very easy to add panic to panic, when sensitization triggers panic so easily.

Naturally panic that comes so easily bewilders the sufferer, and she (here it is a woman) makes the mistake of thinking that it can, of its own accord, grow beyond her control. She does not understand clearly that panic can build up only if she builds it up. By doing as I have taught her so often by taking a deep breath, letting it out slowly, and letting her body slump—whether sitting or standing—and then being willing to let the panic flash, the panic will gradually decrease, and there will never be a "buildup."

So if that woman takes a journey in any vehicle she cannot stop at will, she should start the journey knowing that she will probably panic—fear of it will bring it—but also knowing that if she is prepared to sit and let the panic sweep through her *as willingly as she can manage,* THE PANIC WILL NOT MOUNT. But she must *stay* willing. So many manage to be willing at first, but if panic strikes again too soon after the first flash, they too easily forget willingness and start withdrawing in desperation and fear. Stopping panic from mounting is in everybody's hands by not adding FEAR OF THE PANIC.

I know this sounds simple. It's not simple, and I don't

underestimate the strength of her panic, but she can do it and so can you.

The second part of the experience: suppose she does add panic to panic and the panic mounts; what then? Can there be a crisis so great that she can "go berserk" or "collapse"? There can't. Any movement she makes, no matter what, will thwart any crisis. For example, if she is in a train and gets up in panic and walks out into the corridor, the very getting up and walking defeats the peak of panic so that the moment of crisis passes. Any diversion will blunt the peak of panic. This is a physiological fact. There is no such thing as a continuous crisis. The word *crisis* means a turning point, a peak followed by a falling away. Even if that panicking woman only listens to the man opposite rustling his newspaper, some of her tension goes into listening, and so the peak of that wave of panic passes. No peak goes on peaking continuously at the same level. Peaks always fall away on the other side.

She says she fears she may "go berserk." What does she mean by going berserk? I think she vaguely sees herself running away somewhere, arms waving, even crying out. But that's only hysteria, and with the first burst she'd be so overcome by finding herself in the limelight that the hysteria would fizzle out like a damp firecracker. Such a person is always self-conscious, and if there is one thing a self-conscious person does not do, it's to cry out.

But suppose she breaks all records and does cry out; what then? At the first cry she'd be so overcome with shame that she'd slink back into her seat, and I doubt if she'd have enough strength to panic again on that journey. She is letting the possibility of feeling humiliated before other people—people she'd probably never see again— spoil her life. Wouldn't it be better for her to face the worst bravely and so free herself from her self-created prison? And incidentally, a "worst" that is only part of her imagination. What chains her misty vision is creating!

Also, what does she mean by "collapse"? She doesn't understand collapse clearly either, or she wouldn't use the word. To truly collapse, medically speaking, one's blood pressure must fall dramatically. In a panic blood pressure usually goes up, not down, so how could she collapse? And yet at the moment of peak panic, some people complain that they feel lightheaded or muzzy, as if they are going to collapse. One woman referred to her "blackouts," but when questioned critically, she admitted that she never lost consciousness, only felt that she might. I have been called out to visit a patient whom relatives described as "collapsed," only to have her laughing after a few minutes' talk.

If the woman who wrote that letter did work herself up so that she felt lightheaded and muzzy and then slumped onto the floor with fright and weakness, someone would always help her to her feet again, and she'd always find a good excuse to explain the "collapse."

So what? So what? I wish you would ask yourselves that question. *The courage to go out and face any crisis, whatever it may be, is enough to dampen it.* Can you see that? You are holding only a firecracker (even though it may be a double-bunger!) in your hand and letting that spoil your life!

At a Canadian hospital, a doctor had ballpoint pens stamped with a quote from one of my books, "Recovery lies in the places and experiences you avoid." Never run away from such places or experiences. They are your salvation, because recovery truly lies in them.

So clear away the mists. Understand that the controls are in your hands and that you work those controls by releasing them. Understand that even if you cling on and fail to release them and let panic mount and mount, it can only spend itself in the end. A wave that breaks on the beach, however big, must always recede. Let no vaguely imagined crisis spoil your life.

## KEEP TRUCKING—*October 1979*

Once again I greet you, and once again I have the problem of not knowing how much you personally need this letter and how much you want simply to keep in touch. Because those who need help must be served first I will write as if you, the reader of this letter, are one of them. Many of you are making good progress and may not want to be reminded of the details of your illness, and yet for the sake of others I must give details.

As I have said so often, the most upsetting symptom of sensitized nerves is the intensity of the body's reaction to the slightest anxious thought, and the consequent self-bombardment by fear of this reaction, even to the extent of the sufferer thinking that he, or she, is going mad.

Peace and rest. How they are longed for, and how unattainable they seem. I'm saddened by the number of exhausted people who have no one to turn to for help. I ask, "Isn't there *some* relative or friend with whom you can stay, if only for a little while? Someone who will keep you company during the day and give you a change from loneliness and work?" The answer is so often, "No one!" or, "Only Mum, and she doesn't understand. Anyhow I've worn her out!" One woman, when telephoning me, had to hang up if she heard her husband coming because he was so fed up with her illness. Too often, the way out must be found alone.

Peace lies in finding a satisfactory way of looking at any problem that is helping to keep the sufferer ill, in finding a route to follow (as I have been teaching you), and then, in "keepin' truckin'." Indecision and the bewilderment it brings debilitate, especially if the sufferer is constantly changing his mind and is reacting too intensely to each change. If you suffer this way and understand the effects of sensitization and fatigue and see that it is not necessarily the situation that is causing your present state as much as your too severe reaction to it—especially your reaction to the anxieties and fears associated with it—then, if you can do this, you are on the road to recovery. I know acceptance is very difficult if you live under constant tension at home or at work; but when you do accept (and everybody has the power to do this) your nervous reactions will gradually lessen, your fatigue will lift, and what has seemed impossible for so long gradually will become possible.

But don't try to push yourself to show that you "*can do it!*" Take short rests if necessary. Utter tiredness may be "only nerves," but it feels like utter tiredness just the same. Unfortunately, sleeping during the day can seem more like a nightmare than rest. The fatigued person can wake with such a start (we call this the "startles") that his heart may race and he may feel "flat," depressed, for some hours afterward. If you wake this way, don't think you are uniquely or especially ill. Your body is following an expected pattern that is part of sensitization.

As I have mentioned again and again, having someone with whom to discuss your problem helps tremendously, especially someone who will encourage you. Helpful discussion releases tension, unties the knotted chest, and relaxes the clamped scalp and tight throat. It helps lift the bag of concrete from the heart. However, only too often the sufferer talks indiscriminately to too many people, and some acquaintances not only are unhelpful but have the knack of saying the wrong thing, which sets the sufferer off on another track of misery.

Grotesque, frightening thoughts are not unusual in debilitated people who have no defense against their own imagination—especially fearful imagination. Rest and peace (those beautiful experiences) will come if the sufferer understands and accepts depletion and knows that no devil has him in his power, if he understands that all is caused by sensitization, fatigue, and memory playing their tricks. (But what a devil they can seem! I was too quick saying there was no devil!)

Tranquilizers are sometimes essential, but a wise doctor's direction is necessary.

Change in the pattern of everyday living can act like a mild shock, arresting the sufferer's constant thinking about himself and how he feels. It helps him to suddenly see himself "from the outside," to feel on top of his illness as if detached from it; this enables him to get it into proportion. Simply leaving the house and walking outside can lift the gray veil of mental fatigue a little—if only for a short time. To be able to get away from the house for a month or more is a rare luxury. Most people must stay and recover in the old tracks at home. Recovery is still possible here, but it may take longer.

If you suffer this way, try to see your illness as nervous fatigue from which you will recover if you are willing to accept the strange feelings and sensations, and try to let time pass while waiting for recovery, especially if you are willing to pass through those flash moments when symptoms return so vividly and make you think, all too readily, that you never will be free of them, will never recover.

Let them come, those strange flashes, let all the strange feelings flash back. Even let the stomach churn. Release your tense hold on them and "keep truckin'." But keep trucking willingly, without tensely fighting. And don't keep trying "to get rid of them." No one can get rid of "them" quickly. Only if you work as willingly as you can *with the feelings there* will you gradually be rid of them.

This advice also applies to depressed people. Depression is a chemical disturbance; this is why antidepressants sometimes help. If you are depressed and understand that it is a chemical disturbance and try not to be depressed because you are depressed, your batteries will gradually be recharged; the chemical imbalance will be remedied, and the depression will lift. So be prepared to do things without continually watching to see if you are enjoying doing them. You couldn't suddenly switch from depression to enjoyment, except perhaps for an occasional quick flash.

Also, the last thing you may want to do is to mix with people. It can be almost painful to force your mind to concentrate on what others are saying, and as for sharing their enthusiasm over some everyday happening... ! But *you should mix with people*, however painful it is, and try not to pity yourself too much in the meantime. Try not to gauge your progress by the day or even by the week. Keep trucking, and one morning you will wake without the lump of lead in your stomach, without the rattling heart, and gradually life will be worth living again.

I know this letter applies to only some of you. I apologize to the others. To all of you I send my compassionate understanding and best wishes.

## BREAKING THROUGH THE BARRIER—*July 1980*

Once again I send you my encouragement while you make that steep climb up the slippery slope. Recovery is such a slippery business that I bring you special messages. Some of you may not understand what I'm talking about, but hundreds will, and these may still need a steadying hand.

Recovery can be slow because emotions, felt as intensely as a sensitized person can feel them, can bring some off-putting shocks. The word *shock* may surprise you; however, to the sensitized person a thought or an experience that brings the slightest anxiety or surprise can feel like a physical shock.

For example, as I have mentioned before, a nervously ill person who stays indoors most of the time may be so accustomed to the subdued light inside the house that simply opening the front door to venture out into the bright light can bring such a physical jolt that the would-be adventurer may quickly retreat indoors, defeated.

Again, while recovering, those moments of having a peaceful body may feel so strange that the sudden realization that one's body is at peace may shock, and of course when this happens back come the old fears and bewilderment—plenty of bewilderment. Certainly bewilderment, because where does one go from there? If feeling at peace brings shock, where *does* one go from there?

Even the thought of full recovery may be daunting,

even slightly shocking. The sufferer feels that the vitality demanded by recovery seems beyond his reach. He would almost rather stay ill. He feels he will never be able to make the effort to walk briskly, laugh freely, or talk unselfconsciously. What a mountain to climb, especially when even a peaceful body seems strange. Again, there is recoil in shock.

He asks himself, "How can I, how does anyone, break through such a barrier?" To break through, he *must let the moment of shock pass;* he must pass through, relax through, to the best of his ability, that flash moment of fear and despair and continue with the job on hand. HE MUST PASS THROUGH THAT FRONT DOOR INTO THE BRIGHT LIGHT. Always onward, onward.

With practice at passing through each blow, helped by an understanding that reactions are so severe because of sensitized response, the habit of being balked is gradually replaced by the ability to pass (float, relax, melt) onward, through. When this happens, the shocks come more and more lightly until they NO LONGER MATTER. Finally, they are only a flickering memory, and the barrier is gone.

The way is always onward, through, but there must be no grim fighting. Relaxed acceptance (as much as you can muster) of all obstacles and shocks is the way through. This takes time, courage, patience, perseverance, and picking oneself up from the depths of despair again and again, especially at first, when each blow seems to fall as forcefully as the last, sometimes even more forcefully. But then one day, as I said, comes that wonderful feeling that the shocks no longer matter. Not-mattering is usually fleeting at first—here one moment, gone the next. However, as the blows begin to soften, the former victim begins to feel an inner strength and a feeling that *he* is in charge of the situation at last. He no longer feels buffeted by some strange outside force working within himself. There is no outside force. There are only nerves responding to the stress born of fear, despair, and a body's consequent fatigue. Fatigue can make the way seem especially difficult. Acceptance and understanding gradually lift even fatigue.

I have not forgotten the shocks memory can bring. These are myriad. There are a few people who recover on waves of success and elation. The great majority, however, drag memory and its shocks along with them.

So practice acceptance and always moving onward through all shocks until finally that wonderful moment of not-mattering is permanent. This is how recovery works. Shocks do not disappear by magic. They finally cease coming because EVENTUALLY THEY NO LONGER SHOCK.

Onward, onward, onward, accepting all, however shakily sometimes. Courage, each of you. You have my thoughts, my understanding, and my great sympathy as always.

## WHERE TO FROM HERE?—*July 1982*

Some of you, who have been practicing my teaching for some months and have been successful in moving about your own town—indeed may have achieved much in this way—may now be wondering, "Where do I go from here?" So many have asked me this.

Many of you will remember how happy you were when you made the corner shop, the successful bus ride, the visit to the hairdresser's. That was achievement. Sometimes it brought elation, and relatives and friends, seeing the improvement, may have encouraged you. That was fine.

Your thoughts may now be, "Perhaps if I were to go much further afield—somewhere really challenging—I would be satisfied." But where? There is so little opportunity in ordinary life to go further afield. There's little encouragement to take a long journey to a place you don't know—perhaps just a name on a map, or on the front of a bus—simply to see if "you can do it."

If you were suddenly *obliged* to go to a distant town *that* would be different. There's a real push behind "having to go," and a real push is a wonderful starter. If only the average daily life held more pushes. But it doesn't.

So, with traveling around the hometown conquered, many people begin to worry, because they think they'll never be cured unless they at least have a go at some distant prospect, something that gives them a few cold shivers to contemplate. They don't realize that they could make that heroic effort, that distant journey, successfully and still have within themselves that gnawing, unsatisfied feeling deep of not having achieved enough.

If you are like this, what are you going to do about it? Let me assure you that if you are prepared to continue willingly with your apparently (or, at least, so it seems to you) humdrum living without trying to conquer further fields to convince yourself that you can get there, *you will be recovering all the time*.

Recovery, without your knowledge, is being cemented at your home base by your simply doing the things that come fairly comfortably and perhaps without too much conscious effort on your part. You may be surprised to find that if making some unusually long journey—perhaps an hour or two away from home—is necessary, although you may have plenty of misgivings when you think about it and especially when you start off, all those months of successful (even if only sometimes fairly successful) ordinary living add up, and you will make the journey more easily than you thought possible. Even while you think you are achieving little, you are achieving much. And that is exactly where you go next—to the shops, the school meeting, the hairdresser, and not in your dreams to Land's End or over the Brooklyn Bridge.

You see, two or three long journeys, although exciting and, if successful, very encouraging, can also disappoint because such efforts can only be spasmodic and there is no certainty about spasmodic effort. The only certainty lies within yourself and how you tackle the moments of panic *right on your doorstep*. That is, by seeing panic through until it matters less and less, by going to the other side of panic and finding peace there as I have taught so often. *Going to distant places is not necessary for your recovery.*

While you are coping with yourself in your own home town, you are, at the same time, coping with a distant journey. But you won't be successful in this if you move freely around your own town simply because you have "become used to" doing it. There is no real, permanent peace in getting-used-to. You must have the inner knowledge of going through panic the right way. Only in this way can confidence to face distant journeys be slowly, subconsciously built. Confidence cannot be built successfully unless the foundation is right. If you have come a certain distance by working the right way and are wondering where you go from there, and if you are distressed because nothing far afield offers itself, don't think you won't progress unless you find such a field. You will be getting better all the time if you settle contentedly with what is available at home, provided you are tackling it the right way.

I'll explain again what I mean by recovery. Even when you can do things you previously could not do, memory may sometimes encourage that old demon, panic, to rattle his chains. However, the rattling gradually grows less and less as you cope with it the right way, until it finally fades and is only a thought without too much upsetting bodily reaction. Memory may bring a slight shiver of apprehension (for months, perhaps for years) but what the heck! We can't anesthetize memory.

I don't want to discourage anyone who has his heart set on taking a long journey. If you feel like this you have all my encouragement. So on with your spurs and call for your horse. You'll make it. Remember, you take your cure with you if you loosen and accept.

I am really writing this for the people who have no opportunity to call for a horse. I want to assure them that if they cope with what is at hand the right way, they are coping with that distant journey at the same time. I send you all my encouragement, my thoughts.

# 5

# More Bewilderments Cleared

**Coping with a neighbor.** "How does one cope when out and the neighbor stops to talk and you feel you are going to collapse, or something dreadful is going to happen? What can I do instead of making the usual excuses of, 'I must go. I've left the kettle on!' or, 'I'm waiting for a phone call!'? At home and in the house, I can let go and flop into the chair, but in the street this is impossible. The neighbor may be thinking, 'She's not listening!'

"This makes me dread going out; yet I still go, because I know we have to go into the situations we fear. You say so. You see, I often feel queer before I go out—with lightheadedness, stiff legs, and weakness—yet I know I haven't been anticipating this and once outside, how unreal and strange I feel! Then, if anyone stops me, I've had it!

"I'm the same in the library, if I'm waiting to be served with people behind me. I can't say, 'Just a minute while I try to relax!' I think you understand what I mean. It's so bewildering and makes me feel such a failure, especially when I come home to an empty house with no one to talk to or to encourage me.

"Also, I'm terribly agitated if anyone visits and I don't know them very well. That's a nightmare. The young couple next door asked me in for coffee one day, and a few days later I passed a cup of tea over to them. I said I couldn't go in because I was expecting Bill. I couldn't face the agitation of visiting, although they know I'm not very well."

When you are stopped by a neighbor think to yourself, "Float, just float, float, float! Don't fight!" Take a deep breath, let it out slowly, and at the same time let your body "flop." Your head may feel light, but it won't leave your shoulders! The stiff legs will hold you. These feelings are only tension working its old tricks. You can talk however tense and strange you feel. Your face won't crack if you smile.

If you can't follow every word your neighbor says, say you've got wax in your ears. What the heck! But don't run away to answer that phantom phone. See the talk through as WILLINGLY as you can manage. You'll be surprised what a miracle that old WILLINGLY will work. It begins by stopping that agitated searching for a way to escape.

You don't have to obviously sag or flop (although you probably could do both without the neighbor noticing). It's enough to think, "Float!" and imagine yourself floating, to feel release of some tension.

When you stand in the queue at the library, once again think, "Float, float, float!"

Visiting is always difficult for a nervously ill person. Here is a simple exercise you can do while visiting or being visited: surreptitiously clench one hand as tightly as you can and hold it clenched for about half a minute. When you unclench you will feel some relaxation. I doubt if your companions will be aware of the clenching. The release that follows clenching a hand can also relax tummy muscles.

You haven't been practicing the right way, have you? Are those neighbors in now? How about putting the kettle on?

**Is depression inherited?** In my opinion, depression may not be inherited as much as caused by environment.

104

The mood of one member of a family can be too easily flattened by the depressed attitude of another member. For example, if on waking one is greeted by a cheerful mother, one is much more likely to step out of bed feeling that it's good to be alive than if wakened by a depressed voice that lets one know that life's not worth much anyhow, so why bother?

Also if several members of the family suffer from depression, other members can too easily become afraid that they too will eventually suffer from it. A sure way to become depressed is to be constantly frightened; fear exhausts, and depression is so often an expression of emotional exhaustional.

So if there is more than one member of your family suffering from depression, don't immediately think that you too must inevitably suffer from it. Don't fall into that trap.

**Timing.** I first became aware of the importance of timing while lecturing. I was rushing ahead trying to cram two hours into one. I wanted so earnestly to get the whole message across; I galloped. Suddenly I noticed a restlessness among the audience. I stopped, realized I was going too quickly, took a deep breath, and continued slowly. By rushing I had been confusing them. Better, I thought, to make six points clearly than garble a dozen. The fidgeting stopped. What's more, I fitted in all the points, and my pulse rate settled down.

We can develop our own tranquilization. Some simple kind of meditation in the morning and the afternoon will help to slow down the express train. There is no need to practice a form of meditation with a fancy name; I have my own simple form. For example, I sit quietly, close my eyes, and, with as little thought as possible, listen to outside noises. I used to do this in the middle of a busy office when it was impossible for me to take any other kind of rest. After a few minutes of listening quietly, I felt refreshed, and my pace slowed down.

**How to recognize the beginning of depletion.** A woman wrote: "I have just come through a crisis in my illness. I was greatly helped by your tape on fatigue and realized that I need not feel guilty about my depression and weariness. Sometimes I think that we blame ourselves too much and all that is happening is that our mind is protesting and begging us to let go and, as you say, 'let it all come.' How can we learn to recognize the beginning of depletion? And after we have lived through depletion, how can we avoid it in the future, before it wears us down once more?"

Some of the early symptoms of depletion are difficulty in concentrating, deciding, or remembering; lessened interest; muzzy head; and irritability (too easily aroused emotions). At times there may be a flash of interest, but it soon dies—too much effort! Acting on an idea is difficult.

However, one must remember that before depletion there must be much stress. Depletion does not follow physical work. It depends on glandular exhaustion, and physical work does not exhaust glands—only stress or disease can do that.

Living always on guard against depletion means being unnecessarily tense, and this would soon invite fatigue, the forerunner of depletion. Better to arrange one's life sensibly within one's capacity and then forget about "guarding against depletion," at the same time, remembering that how much one does is not as important as how one does it. If you are the kind of person who rushes through "jobs to be done," practice timing. When you forget and do rush (as we all do at times), at least don't fret because you are rushing.

It's the anxiety added to fatigue that prolongs fatigue. Fatigue, even emotional and mental fatigue, will heal if we don't interfere by becoming anxious about it.

Often we get more relaxation by changing our work than by stopping working. Working with one's hands is a restful change for those who work constantly with their brain. The housewife may groan when she reads this because relaxation for her would be to forget that she had hands. For relaxation, she can lower her standards; if the beds aren't made on time, or even aren't made at all, so what?

**Talking to others about frightening thoughts.** Some ask if talking to others about their frightening thoughts is "not accepting."

Putting thoughts into words so often robs them of importance—they can suddenly seem silly. So talking about frightening thoughts *to a suitable confidant* can be good therapy. The confidant should be one who realizes the unimportance of the thoughts (although they may sound bloodcurdling!) and who doesn't withdraw in shock and say, "You'll have to be careful, Willy, you could be going silly!" Not that kind of confidant.

During early stages in nervous illness, comforting words from others can sometimes break tension quicker than one's own anxious, desperate effort at self-comfort.

One woman found relief by saying to a particular friend, "Please, Jean, repeat what I say to you." Just hearing her own words coming from another's lips (even from someone who didn't quite understand the meaning of the words) had more impact than saying them herself.

Hearing wise advice from cassettes can help those who have no confidant.

**Battening down a vivid imagination.** "How can I batten down a vivid imagination?"

Don't try to. Give it full reign, but remember that it is only imagination. It is not a question of dampening a vivid imagination to gain peace but one of robbing imagination of its power to frighten. As one man put it, "Recovery begins when the stupidities no longer matter." One's imagination can certainly bring stupidities. Better to accept stupidities than try to batten imagination down!

While we try to batten down a few stupidities, they

turn into rabbits, and we finish trying to batten down dozens. Let them all come; invite them all. Unwanted thoughts dislike being invited to the party so much, they rarely come.

**Occupation and depression.** I was talking to a group of nervously ill people in England and noticed a woman sitting quietly in one corner. She seldom spoke. Her husband had died six months previously, and she had but one daughter who lived in London. She was quiet because she was so depressed. Each day was a burden. The housework was done by early morning and then the long empty hours lay ahead.

When the group began discussing how they would help her to be occupied, her face lit up and she came to life. The promise of work did more for that woman than all the antidepressant drugs and tranquilizers she had taken.

When suitable occupation in the company of other people is found for lonely or depressed people, such medication can often be washed down the sink.

**Not again!** "It's difficult in setback to remember how well I felt when I was making good progress. How can I shorten the time in a setback? I get feelings like, 'I can't go through all that first-line battle stuff again! I really can't!' But I do go through it."

It's difficult in setback to remember how well one recently felt, because setback itself brings such disappointment. Also, nervous feelings seem to be so much more acute when they have been absent for some time. So much of their sting may have been forgotten that when it returns it can shock!

Shock, fear, exasperation, and despair are so normal in setback they are even part of recovery! I like my patients to have setbacks and the experience of learning how to come out of them. The experience gained in coming through each setback absorbs some of the shock of

future setbacks and brings heart-warming encouragement.
So welcome setback, don't shrink from it.

**Rooted to the ground.** "When I have to stand still
even for a short time, I feel as if my feet are rooted to the
ground and my body is swaying about."

Severe tension can bring a feeling of being "rooted to
the ground." Trying to force a way forward does not
help—it acts like a clamp. The answer is to float, not fight.
Simply thinking of floating can relax and loosen, and a
loosened body can move.

One of my patients—a violinist who hadn't worked for
two years—on recovering, was very anxious to get back to
playing on the stage. He accepted an engagement and
after finishing his solo bowed and turned to leave. He
couldn't budge. His right foot was clamped to the floor. He
began to panic and thought, "What would Dr. Weekes say
now? She'd say float, so I've got to float!" But he couldn't
move his foot. It was clamped to the floor by a ball of
chewing gum. Floating can dissolve tension, but not
gum.

**Fear of open heights.** Many people are afraid of
them. To look down many stories over an open balcony
needs nerve and a strong stomach. I always get a clutching
hand in mine. Treating such dislike is comparable to
treating dislike of being in an elevator. I never worry my
patients about trying to overcome fear of elevators unless
they need to use them often and the alternative is climbing
long flights of stairs.

However, fear of open heights can be embarrassing,
for example, when visiting a friend in his penthouse. So
here's a suggestion (I do this myself): as you look over the
balcony (or cliff edge or whatever) take the usual deep
breaths, let them out very slowly, and really *look* down
with open eyes and head forward—no head-back, narrow-
eyed look! Doing this, I can even look out the window of a
plane as it banks to land.

**An adequate medical examination.** I have sometimes been asked by a nervously ill person what I consider
to be an adequate examination. When I was a general
practitioner, an adequate examination meant asking a patient to remove most of his clothes and then examining
him on the couch: his hair, eyes, tongue, mouth, palpating
the neck, looking at the hands, feeling the pulse, listening
to the heart and chest, palpating the breasts and abdomen,
testing arteries in legs and feet, examining reflexes, taking
blood pressure, and examining urine. Any further tests
made would depend on the results of such an examination.
That would be an adequate examination and would not
take so long if practiced often enough to become routine.

**Blood pressure tablets.** I am writing this short warning because the dose prescribed (especially of a beta-
blocker) for so many people with high blood pressure is
too heavy. On a too heavy dose, they can feel apathetic,
lethargic, even depressed or have "weak turns," dragging,
heavy legs, and a tendency to stagger. They can also have
pains and a feeling of weakness across the chest—mimicking
angina. Too often the victim mistakes these symptoms for
"a bad heart" and suffers unnecessarily while he drags
himself from day to day.

Because beta-blockers slow the heart rate, they are
sometimes prescribed for the anxiety state. Obviously the
dose should be carefully monitored; otherwise it could
complicate rather than help.

**Upsetting irritation: thumping on the bed!** A man
wrote, "A friend visited me while I was ill. As he talked he
thumped the end of my bed with his fist—a heavy thump.
Should I have put up with this (accepted it), or should I
have told him to please stop? Would that have been
running away, not accepting?"

It would have been wisdom, not running away. There's
no need to be martyred unnecessarily. When sensitized (as
this man was) nervous reaction to an irritant can be

extreme. If a thumping fist (dripping tap, ticking clock, talkative neighbor) can't be stopped, try relaxing toward it and actually listening to it. This works.

**After the birth of my baby!**  So many mothers say, "It all began after the birth of my baby!" Sometimes the exertion of childbirth, with the possible upset in glandular balance, and the work and loss of sleep a new baby entails are enough to lead to depletion and depression.

Any mother, when depleted, can become afraid of harming her children—especially a young baby, so trusting, so dependent. The thought can naturally flash into the tired mind, "Wouldn't it be awful if I hurt my baby!" And even, "Perhaps I really would!"

Unfortunately, some of these mothers are told by their therapists that they are aggressive types. They are *not* aggressive types; they are simply passing through an obsessive phase that anyone could have in similar circumstances. Once more, cure lies in glimpsing the obsession as ONLY A THOUGHT IN A TIRED MIND MAKING AN EXAGGERATED IMPRESSION ON A SENSITIZED BODY.

**Dreading hot weather.**  Dilation of blood vessels in hot weather (to allow cooling) can bring symptoms similar to those of nervous illness: flushed face, throbbing head, sweating, perhaps thumping heart and even fatigue. These symptoms may dupe a nervously fatigued or nervously ill person into thinking that his nerves are once more "in a bad way." Even if he finally understands the cause—hot weather—he may come to so dread the heat that he encourages the symptoms.

Some nervously ill people complain that cold weather also increases awareness of nervous symptoms. The effects of weather, hot or cold, should be understood, and since we can't change the weather, we know what to do!

**A husband's help.**  A woman who had been agoraphobic for 12 years asked if she would ever function on her own without her husband's help. Answer: she won't until she tries. Twelve years is a long time to be without confidence. To change that situation she must change herself—and soon. She must not wait for confidence to come to her; it won't.

She must face taking those first tottering steps holding her own hand, not her husband's! And she must try not to be too discouraged by failure. Of course, she will fail sometimes, so why waste time being impressed by it?

She must practice, practice, practice, the way I have consistently taught her in my books (for her, especially *Simple, Effective Treatment of Agoraphobia*) and cassettes (again, for her, the cassette *Moving to Freedom,* in which I go through panic with her). It's all there. At least when she decides to practice without her husband, she will be pointing herself in the right direction at last: toward recovery.

**Living with a nervously ill relative.**  People who live with a nervously ill relative need short spells away from the tension. It's useless to simply keep making and breaking resolutions about being patient. The binding tension that can follow no more than a plaintive request from the sick relative can shatter all such resolutions. Spells away, however short, are the remedy, although they are more easily prescribed than obtained.

**Fear of illness.**  Most people neither become seriously ill nor die young. So the odds are in our favor. However, no nervously ill person should live in anxious doubt about his health. He should immediately consult his doctor about any suspicious symptom and so get peace of mind, and he must not think that by doing this he is being hypochondriacal. He is being sensible.

Also, the death we fear when young may hold no fears as we grow older. When old, simply doing the ordinary jobs that mean living can become an effort, and so death gradually loses its terror; indeed, to many it may seem like a release. Even the manner of dying need not be feared. I have seen so many die peacefully, unaware that they were dying. When my mother was ill, my brothers and their children came to see her, and afterward she laughingly said, "The old sillies! My birthday was last Saturday, not today!" She didn't realize she was ill, and yet she died that same week. She had said to me some years earlier, "I am not afraid of dying. I am just a little afraid of how I will die." She died in her sleep. So don't waste the young years worrying about the old years to come.

**How will I know when I'm cured?** When you can live in peace with the memory of what you have been through and if, when times of stress bring back your old symptoms, you can accept these and not let them upset you too much, not let them disrupt your life, then you can say you are cured.

Of course, being cured does not mean having a constantly peaceful body. Life must always hold some stress to which one's body may respond with some upsetting symptoms, so don't search for the impossible—calm, perfect calm, always!

Recovery means that although symptoms can return under stress, there is a deep inner feeling of peace because the symptoms have come to no longer matter. Nothing can completely take away this feeling, and it comes only when past successful experiences have become your insulation against despair. In other words, you may have to come through setbacks successfully many times before you can finally face one calmly, knowing so well how to cope with it because *it no longer matters!*

**Constant nausea.** Treating constant nausea is difficult, because so often it is the result of constant anxiety. When the mind is at peace nausea can go surprisingly quickly. A chronically nauseated, nervously ill woman under great stress was persuaded to take a holiday. She said that from feeling too nauseated to even look at food, she ate hungrily on the airplane. From then on during the holiday she ate well, with no nausea. However, on the return plane journey the nausea returned. This showed her clearly how closely it was related to stress.

Of course, not everyone can have a holiday to relieve nausea; however, there are a few other remedies to try. First, check constipation; this occurs frequently in nervous illness, when the sufferer is too agitated to take enough time on the toilet and perhaps does not drink enough fluid or eat much food.

In nervous illness the tongue may be coated and sour (often aggravated by tranquilizers). The tongue should be cleaned with a soft toothbrush and then the mouth cleansed with a mild mouthwash: glycothymol works well and is pleasant.

If the doctor has prescribed a tranquilizer for nausea, it should be taken half an hour before the main meal.

A nervously ill person should not try to face a big meal sitting with the family. He usually has more success managing a small meal in private (if this can be arranged). Eating with others at the table, especially if the conversation is noisy, demands a great deal of effort from a very tired person. Also, instead of facing a set meal, it may be less effort to nibble at food during the day: a dish of nuts, fruit, dried fruit, cubes of cheese, biscuits, and so on, in different rooms. Of course, there is the old standby—egg and milk beaten together with added flavoring.

If the nervously ill person is eating poorly, vitamin supplements are essential, but not in massive doses. Too many can be as dangerous as too few; for example, too much vitamin $B_1$ can overstimulate.

Tablets are prescribed for nausea; for example, thiethylterazime (called Torecan in Australia). Unfortunately antinausea tablets can sometimes cause drowsiness. The good news is that when stress goes, nausea goes with it. I do not worry my patients about low-cholesterol diets while they're trying to recover an appetite. Even when well, moderation in all things!

**Unnecessary worry.** Carrying worry around is a hang-over from the time when there was too much genuine worry, perhaps a too rapid succession of worries.

The effects of worry can vary from a tension headache to being simply a dull, rather muzzy feeling in the head, rather like a threatening headache. One woman said that although she knew there was nothing now to worry about, she still played the "worry record" and felt sure that if she searched diligently enough she'd find some worry somewhere.

The worry habit is encouraged by staying indoors too much. Sometimes to simply walk through the front door into the light, into activity, is enough to alert the worrier to the grayness of the worry cloud enveloping him. He can then appreciate that his worry is a physical state rather than a reality.

While such small shocks help, bigger shocks (like going on holiday) help even more. Tension is eased and a habit broken.

For "chronic worriers" who cannot have a holiday I recommend working outdoors; the feeling of space above can lift the pressing ceiling of worry tension.

**Tension and obsession.** "When I am with my doctor, I can relax and believe all is right—that I will never harm anyone willfully—but when I leave him the obsession returns."

When the doctor relieved her tension and she re-laxed, she could think more flexibly—think "around corners" —and see her obsession as simply an idea that she could dismiss.

Although temporarily eased by the doctor, the tension underlying obsession is great indeed and could grip with its old force as soon as this woman thought again, as she invariably must, of the obsession. Indeed, tension could grip before she left the doctor's office. She would probably then think, "Oh God! Here it is again! And after all the doctor said! There's no hope for me!"

The return of an obsession when it is thought to have been lost, can bring shock that feels like a physical blow. A doctor should explain this. Understanding obsession and how it works and then practicing "glimpsing" can save months of suffering and finally cure. I described "glimpsing" in chapter 3.

**How to know when you are normal?**   "I have been nervously ill since childhood, so how will I know when I'm better? I don't know what being normal means; most people aim to be as they were, but I have no guidelines."

This woman should work on without analyzing her feelings too closely, without considering whether they are normal or not, without wondering, "Now what did they mean by that?" or "What did I mean by that? Was that a normal reaction?" She must try not to be critical of her reactions; she should give them the signal "Full steam ahead!"

Being normal simply means her being less self-critical, less self-aware, and more at ease with people. As she goes forward without too much introspection, normality will embrace her gently. She will be at ease.

She can take heart. Few nervously ill people remain as they were before their illness. Character strengthens as difficulties are overcome. Recovery is a new experience for all.

So this woman need not worry about recognizing normality in herself. She should not try to search for it but should live from day to day, letting normality come to her. She will recognize it because she will gradually feel less tense and more at ease.

**Going for a job.**   Should a person who has recovered from nervous illness mention the past when being interviewed for a job? A woman recently telephoned from the United States saying that although she was a good floral arranger (she had owned her own shop), she could not get a job in her hometown because rumors about her

116

having been nervously ill had spread quickly in the florist world. She said that for the first few days in a new job all would be well; then the freeze would start. Unfortunately, few people can understand nervous illness until they have experienced it.

Having been nervously ill is a very private affair, so keep it private when you apply for a job. You need not feel guilty. Experience gained in recovering the hard way—and mine is the hard way—builds character. Anyone can be tricked into becoming nervously ill; often it's just chance that some are and some aren't.

If we talked more freely about nervous illness, how much less mysterious it would be! There is no bogeyman manipulating people into "it," only certain natural laws working automatically, laws that can be reversed when we know how to reverse them. So don't feel guilty when you keep your business to yourself; perhaps feel just a little wiser, more mature, than those around.

**Wishing it would all go away.** "I wish it would all go away. I'm tired of battling with these thoughts!"

There is no "it"; there is only his habit of thinking, grooved by mental fatigue. What he tries to forget one minute, habit and fatigue will present again the next. Although he can switch attention if something important demands it, when the demand passes he quickly remembers the "battling" and is caught once more in the old habit.

I repeat again and again that recovery lies in accepting strange thoughts as part of ordinary thinking—especially repeated thought. Constant repetition can itself be upsetting, although the thought may not be strange.

This man should not think, "I mustn't think that!" and then shy away from the thoughts, hoping they will go. He must understand that in his present state of self-awareness he hasn't a hope of forgetting them. He should relax toward them, think them willingly. When he does this, tension will ease, the "grooves" melt, and the habit gradually lift. This is the only way.

**Stopping "horrible" thoughts about loved ones.** "My psychologist said I must stop these horrible thoughts coming. Is that the way to deal with my problem?"

No. While this man fears these thoughts so much, how can he stop them? He should, as I advise so often, understand that THEY ARE ONLY THOUGHTS, HOWEVER HORRIBLE, and let them come.

The writer of the letter added that the thoughts were about those he loved and that it hurt very much to know that he could think this way.

So many nervously ill people have the most bizarre thoughts particularly about those they love, because this hurts most, and in a state of sensitization and fatigue, a sufferer may deliberately probe to see how horrible his thoughts can be. This is common in nervous illness; it seems part of an expected pattern. Its only significance is that the sufferer, being so suggestible, can't resist testing his own suggestibility. How cruelly can he think? How crazy can he be? How much more is there to be frightened of?

As I say so often, a person suffering this way should practice seeing his thoughts for what they are: thoughts established, not because of their truth, but because of the intense, fearful reaction they bring to a sensitized body. And he should understand that they may return from time to time even after he has lost fear of them. Habits take time to break. But when thoughts no longer matter, what harm if they do sometimes return?

With acceptance the time comes when the sufferer suddenly thinks gleefully, "The darn things don't matter any more! They just don't matter! It doesn't matter whether I think them or not!" We lose upsetting thoughts *by drawing their teeth, not by trying to stop their biting.*

**Group therapy.** I've been communicating with groups of nervously ill people in Australia, Great Britain, America,

Africa, and Canada. Many members seem satisfied with their group and are making progress. Yesterday, the organizer of a group telephoned and said that her members inspired each other to get moving and that the progress of some was incredible.

Provided a group has positive-minded members, it can give great support and motivation, especially to lonely people. A group of pessimists who "can't do this" and "can't do that" is of little help. The majority of group members I have met are optimists; however, if you join a group, don't feel obliged to stay with it if you find it unsatisfactory.

Anyone considering starting a group should be on guard against feeling power. It's so easy to feel power when at the head of a group of nervous, vulnerable, suggestible, nervously ill people. The leader of a group should always stay humbled by his own experiences and always see himself or herself as a friend and helper, never as a particularly gifted therapist and certainly never as God. One therapist said to me, "How do you stop yourself from feeling like God?" I think that illustrates my meaning. Beware of that trap.

**Can we forgive ourselves?** The nearest we can come to forgiving ourselves is to realize that we are different now from that person who transgressed and that we would not make the same mistake today. Life demands mistakes and demands that we remember them.

So we must be philosophical about our past mistakes. And that is about as close as any of us can get to forgiving ourselves.

**Recovered from nervous illness but not enjoying living alone or going out.** Living alone is difficult for some (it's not easy to laugh on one's own!) and for a person who has been nervously ill it can be especially difficult because she (a woman made this complaint) may still carry "the shadow of the shadow"—a mixture of memory and some leftover depletion.

Also, she may feel cheated of time by her illness and may, when out, be too aware of needing to enjoy herself, of having to make up for all those lost months. So she may try too hard, perhaps expect too much.

Nature will restore vitality in her own time, if this woman cooperates by not trying for enjoyment too earnestly and is prepared to let more time pass and not watch her progress too closely while she waits.

**Why do things look different?** "Why is it that when I visit a familiar place—but perhaps not seen for some time—it looks and seems different, although it hasn't really changed? I keep saying to whoever's with me, 'Does it look different to you? Are you sure it doesn't look different?'"

A nervously ill person lives so much in his own thoughts that when he visits a place he has not seen for some time, this change in his surroundings can almost forcibly draw him out of himself, make him notice the outside world. This experience is the strangeness he feels, not so much the place. For a moment everything may look clean, almost "just washed"—certainly different—because he's probably looking at it intently for the first time in months.

This is all part of recovery. Isn't that good?

**Is there a complete cure?** It would surely be difficult for a nervously ill person to suffer as he has and not sometimes recoil at the memory. For as long as memory brings suffering, doubting complete recovery is natural.

Recovery means being able to look full-faced at memory, prepared to accept any suffering it may bring. Complete cure does not necessarily mean absence of symptoms, although it can. It means knowing how to cope with the symptoms stress may present, at any time, any place.

Being able to cope is not only possible, it is inevita-

120

ble, when recovery has been earned by the sufferer's own effort based on understanding.

**Hypoglycemia.** During the last decade some therapists have stressed the importance of hypoglycemia in causing nervous illness. I have seen it do this occasionally. An unsuspecting and normally healthy person, after eating little breakfast, could have a spell of weakness, trembling, perhaps sweating before lunch and mistakenly think he is about to die or at least have a heart attack. Unless the innocence of the attack were explained to him, he could perhaps become afraid of going out alone "for fear of having a spell" and so perhaps develop agoraphobia.

Hypoglycemia means low blood sugar—too little glucose in the blood. Glucose is our source of energy, so naturally with too low a supply we can feel all the symptoms mentioned above.

But, while blood may not have enough glucose, the liver has it stored as glycogen, which it breaks down into glucose to meet the blood's demand; so that rest alone (while the liver does its work) will remedy low blood sugar.

However, the sufferer wants quick relief (before he "dies"!), and this comes with eating. The instinct is to reach for something sweet; however, protein (for example, a piece of cheese or a banana) should be the main choice supplemented with a *little* sugar. Too much sugar stimulates the pancreas to secrete more insulin, and so the attack may recur later.

Hypoglycemia is not serious in a normally healthy person, and many, many people have had at least one attack. Some causes are (1) not enough protein for breakfast—the dashed-off cup of coffee, slammed front door, the "shakes" before lunch (the "I never eat breakfast" syndrome); (2) stress stimulating the pancreas to excessive secretion of insulin (anyone under stress, especially the nervously ill, can have attacks of hypoglycemia even soon after a meal—this can puzzle the sufferer; he need wonder no longer); (3) a diet too rich in sugar—this also over-stimulates the pancreas to secrete insulin; (4) being prediabetic or diabetic; (5) postoperative—an operation on the stomach in particular; (6) diseases of the pancreas.

A nervously ill person reading this could immediately think, "Perhaps I have a disease of my pancreas or am diabetic!" To ease these fears he should have his urine tested for glucose. The five-hour glucose tolerance test is very popular today; however, recognizing that stress can stimulate secretion of insulin and cause hypoglycemia, a simple urine test for glucose is, in my opinion, adequate for a nervously ill person who fears diabetes. Tape for testing is sold by the pharmacist.

**Relaxing mentally.** "You say so often 'loosen and accept,' and I can loosen physically by taking deep breaths and letting them out slowly and then by relaxing my muscles, particularly chest and abdominal muscles. This I do conscientiously and deliberately. But how do I loosen mentally? I know that physical relaxation helps to relax mentally, but what can I do *mentally* to bring loosening? What thoughts should I think to be able to relax mentally?"

Feeling constant "mental tension," despite attempts at physical relaxation, sends so many reaching for a tranquilizer, a cigarette, or alcohol. Tension from stress can be so severe that the slightest touch of extra tension (perhaps a mere flicker of anxiety) can put muscles into a binding clinch: the iron band around the scalp. The iron band is sometimes mistaken for mental tension because it seems to tighten further with each stressful thought.

When this man asks what to think to help him loosen mentally, he really means what to think to lessen muscular tension that feels like mental tension. There is no such thing as mental tension.

Some people have described how, when in a moment of what they called "great mental tension," their thoughts have seemed to recede to the back of their head—back, back, back! They thought that if they did not hold on grimly and resist that backward drift, they would go "over the edge" and never come back. They were never sure where they would recede to because their imagination balked at looking clearly over that edge, where they suspected insanity might lie. Few realized they were feeling no more than a severe spasm of muscular tension. Brains may seem dull or muzzy, but they do not tense.

This man is really asking what he should think about in order to comfort himself and so help his muscles relax. If he is upset only by "the state he is in"—that is, of his continually waking early and feeling fearful for no special reason (as I suspect)—I suggest that he switch on the light and read this book. There should be comfort here.

**Will I faint?** The fear of fainting haunts many nervously ill people. When questioned, they admit that although they have "felt like it," they have never actually fainted.

What is so terrible about fainting? I've done it many times. It seems to be my reaction to intense physical pain. However, I can always manage to find a safe place to fall before I go right off; ringing in the ears gives a good warning.

For some nervously ill, there is the added fear of "making a scene" in front of other people. What matter if people see one faint? All the better: there'll be someone there to help, if help is needed. Actually, little help is needed, because in the horizontal (fainting) position, circulation rights itself and the victim revives.

On questioning nervously ill people who say that they have fainted, I usually find some contributing cause; for example, they may have been standing still for a long time. A fall in blood supply to the brain can cause fainting.

If only the nervously ill person who fears fainting could faint and get it over! Familiarity breeds contempt, even of fainting. It's the great unknown that frightens. And, as I mentioned earlier, before fainting one usually has enough warning to position oneself safely. Once, when

I was about to faint, a friend with me said, "Quickly, tell me what I have to do! I haven't a clue!" I had time to tell her to do nothing.

**A binding awareness of self: inward thinking.** A person may have recovered from much of his nervous illness to find that he has developed a consciousness of himself—of his thoughts and actions—that bewilders, alarms, and exhausts. He delays his own recovery by a too fierce, too tense recoil from this self-awareness; he feels imprisoned within himself and makes the mistake of struggling to be free, trying to force self-forgetfulness.

Little can be forced successfully in nervous illness, least of all forgetfulness of self. The only way to lose this inward thinking (as I call it) is *not* to recoil from it, *to let it come and accept it as part of ordinary thinking;* to accept it as part of ordinary, normal awareness, however stifling it may seem, however "crazy," devastating, exhausting, or frightening. ACCEPT IT ALL. WORK WITH IT THERE, WILLINGLY!

I know that some fear that if they do this they will become more firmly entrenched in the habit. THEY WON'T, I ASSURE THEM.

If they let inward thinking (and this includes self-awareness) come with utter acceptance, the habit will gradually lose its significance, and *they will be free*. I do not mean that they will never think inwardly—we all do unconsciously some of the time—but they will not see it as unusual or frustrating. Its presence will not matter any more.

If a former sufferer has been free of inward thinking (especially for a long time), and then one day feels menaced by its return, he should try not to recoil in shock. Once more he should relax, go toward it, and let it come, remembering that if he does this with utter acceptance, the habit will once more "mizzle" as it did in the past.

A student described his sudden insight into inward thinking. One evening, a neighbor stood talking to him while standing in the doorway swinging a lantern. As the student watched the man's mouth move and the lantern swing, his thoughts, as usual, kept reverting to himself. He was so distraught by this that he hardly heard what the man was saying. Then suddenly his thoughts seemed to revert more lightly, with less tension. He thought, "It doesn't really matter what I think when I do this! I could just as well keep thinking 'Tick!' This is only a habit of thinking back to myself. Only a habit!" He said it was almost as if a light suddenly shone in the room, and his spirits leaped as he realized that any outside interest would be enough to free him from the habit.

The next day when the habit returned he said it seemed as if a gray curtain would descend for a while and then lift again. He recognized the curtain as fatigue and was elated, because during the moment of its lifting he could glimpse so well that he would recover. A few days later some friends in another state invited him to visit them, and he knew that if he accepted the change, the curtain would lift very quickly and would stay lifted. He chose to remain where he was, working on his own with his thoughts on himself. He wanted to prove to himself that he could recover without distraction. He wanted to know that if the habit returned in the future, he would not have to depend on change or diversion to lose it again. He stayed and proved his point. He had released the tension that bound his thoughts to himself. He had "rolled with the punches" and recovered.

Some therapists' ignorance of inward thinking is tragic because, as I have explained, it can be cured. A lecturer at an Australian university treated a woman with inward thinking for two years. He used psychoanalysis. Finally he told her he could neither understand her condition nor cure her. However, he said that an American psychiatrist would be visiting the university and that he might be able to help her. After treating her for six months, this visiting doctor said, "I don't understand your illness either!" This ignorance was tragic because it meant years of unnecessary suffering for her. She was finally cured by the understanding and acceptance I taught her.

**Flatulence may not be nervous.** "I have suffered from flatulence since childhood, but it has worsened during the last years. I am now 70. I have most of the other symptoms of nervous depletion. I faithfully carry out your directions of facing, accepting, floating, and letting time pass, but I still suffer from flatulence.

"The doctors at the hospital say there is no physical reason and that I am a wind swallower. They offer no cure. One suggested that I hold a cork between my teeth after each meal. This, they said, would prevent me from swallowing air. I've tried this for a long time, and it doesn't work. I have wind continually whatever I eat and however much I chew my food. So I have begun to think it must be nervous."

So many doctors talk about wind swallowing. People don't swallow wind for the fun of it; they do it mainly because their stomach feels uncomfortable. In my opinion, the discomfort comes first and brings the urge to swallow. Certainly swallowing air increases discomfort, which again encourages more swallowing. Holding a cork between the teeth after meals is a favorite and futile prescription, which leads only to a lot of dribbling and more discomfort. What is one supposed to do with the dribble if not swallow it? And with it, more air!

The causes of flatulence are so many that it's daunting to begin to discuss them. In middle-aged and older people, perhaps one of the commonest causes is esophageal reflux. As we age, the normally tight sphincter between our swallowing tube (esophagus) and our stomach may become lax, especially if we are overweight, so that when we stoop—for example, to tie our shoes or clean the bath—the acid contents of our stomach may rise into our esophagus and cause heartburn. If the area (at the base of the breastbone) is frequently bathed with acid it may become inflamed and hurt as food passes through it, especially "acid" or spicy food: curry, pineapple, fruit cake, tomatoes, alcohol, carbonated drinks, and so on.

Flatulence can be nervous. Our stomach is our most sympathetic organ; it weeps when other organs are in trouble. So, to treat nervous flatulence, any outstanding problem should be resolved if possible. This can be difficult in one's seventies. That peaceful old age we are promised when young is a mirage for many. Old age can bring so many problems—and when we feel too tired to cope!

So, while flatulence can certainly be nervous, there are many other organic causes that should be checked.

# 6

# Talks with Patients

## FIRST PATIENT

WATCHING FOR THE BUILDUP.   A nervously ill person is greatly influenced by his mood of the moment because his body reacts so quickly and so acutely to it. The man in the following interview said he'd had a wonderful day, got up next morning, and still felt wonderful but that when he turned to open a window—flash! Unreality smote! He couldn't work this out. He'd gone to bed feeling peaceful and had wakened peaceful, so why the sudden flash?

He did not realize that underneath the feeling of peace, his body was still sensitized and nervously fatigued. Physically damaged nerves can take up to six months to heal, so why shouldn't sensitized nerves take time also? They do. His nerves were still ready to respond too quickly and too intensely to the slightest shock—even a sudden turn that may have brought a feeling of "floatiness" in the head.

At the time of this experience, this man was on holiday. His nerves had felt peaceful during the day he mentioned because nothing had occurred to aggravate them or test them; but as soon as he got a slight shock (he may have turned to the window very quickly) sensitization reared its head and showed itself in a flash. Nervous illness takes a lot of understanding, doesn't it? Recovery is a question of enough time passing for habit and reaction to lose their grip.

The same man said he could be under enormous tension at the office with his head feeling as if pressed in a vise and yet, if something caught his attention, even though it brought tense concentration, the viselike grip would ease and the tension disappear. But, although he was no longer so afraid of the symptoms of nervous illness, he still watched for the "buildup," especially the brain fag.
*The patient (the same man):* "Doctor, although I'm getting better I have a funny lost feeling. How can this be, when I know I'm recovering?"
*Doctor:* "You feel lost because you are no longer constantly occupied with watching your symptoms and worrying about them. It's a long time since you had no symptoms to worry about; of course you will feel strange for a while."
*Patient:* "It's interesting that although I'm no longer as afraid of the symptoms, I still watch for that buildup, especially the brain fag part."
*Doctor:* "The brain fag comes very quickly at the moment."
*Patient:* "Within seconds."
*Doctor:* "Looking for a buildup is part of recovery. This is why so many feel bewildered by recovery."
*Patient:* "I can understand people fighting against it, because when the feeling comes I feel as if I will be lost forever unless I do fight it."
*Doctor:* "Don't try to keep a 'hold' on yourself. You don't come back to being yourself that way. Let go and float up. I say *up* to, not *back* to, because always remember you go forward, forward in thought, never backward. Never try to scramble back to where you think you were before you were ill, or even before you had a particular setback. Always float forward, always onward. Trying to get back is like Lot's wife. Beware that pillar of salt.

"Also, instant recovery from nervous illness is very rare (although I have seen it). Usually you have to pack in much more normal living before you can feel normal and know that the feeling is established, not just grasped momentarily. You need so much ordinary living to be able to relax in it with assurance. Time must pass; always give it time.

"In the beginning when you first have moments of feeling normal, this feeling can be mixed with other emotions, even elation, and this can be a trap. While you feel elated you can suddenly switch to feeling abnormal again because, naturally, you feel strange feeling elated! It may be a long time since you felt normal, so the feeling may seem strange, even abnormal."

*Patient:* "You're right, doctor. When I'm happy, for instance, at the club, I suddenly think, 'I shouldn't feel like this!' And I almost feel guilty because I'm feeling well. So my heart sinks again and there seems no way out.

"And yet I'm feeling so much better. I'm not overreacting the way I was. I'm floating up gently. The funny thing is, I'm even a bit afraid to be happy about that!"

*Doctor (laughing):* "You become too excited and your mind switches back immediately to your illness, when you were agitated, and you feel drawn back into the quagmire. Don't be oppressed by this; don't be oppressed by the strangeness of any feeling, particularly of feeling happy. It must feel strange. Pass through, on. Recognize feeling guilty because you are happy as one of those flash moments through which you must always pass."

*Patient:* "I think this feeling of being lost is mostly when I'm tired and can't talk to myself convincingly."

*Doctor:* "You are right. Your body has responded to anxiety too intensely for so long that you have to be only mildly anxious now to feel a strong undercurrent of apprehension.

"You may ask yourself what on earth you are anxious about and will you ever stop apprehending. It's difficult to believe you will, but living with utter acceptance of all the strangeness will eventually bring enough relaxation and freedom from stress to finally bring peace. So, on your way!"

**A later session with the same patient.** *Patient:* "It's so difficult to stay peaceful, even when I know what to do!"

*Doctor:* "To recover, you have to accept that the human body is like a machine. It is fantastic and works marvelously for us; however, it can be strained by too heavy a load. Although you said that in your youth you felt like a god, eager to achieve, your body knew you were achieving the wrong way—too much impetuous ardor, not enough balance, not enough time for contemplation or rest. Too much 'On Stanley, on!' If you are prepared to accept that even *you* have a limit, you will be ready to listen and learn. Also, there is a way to placate your hurt ego. You can think, 'I'm going to become a better fellow out of this!' What's more, you will be."

*Patient:* "Does depression come out of being so concerned with oneself?"

*Doctor:* "Depression is a form of exhaustion. When anxious self-concern is frequent it is certainly exhausting and so can bring depression. If you were consistently concerned about someone else, you could also become emotionally drained and consequently depressed. Normally we keep our stores of vitality replenished by day-to-day uplifting experiences; but when nervously depleted, our feelings are not as easily uplifted, so we miss this daily recharging. It's like a car: if the battery is used too much, the headlights and starter fail. Our battery can be depleted in so many ways. We can leave the switch on while we toss and turn at night worrying because we are not getting enough sleep to be ready for tomorrow."

*Patient:* "How do you explain the peace of mind I had last night? I went to bed at 2:30 A.M. I lay peacefully in bed and was asleep in five minutes. I woke at eight this morning feeling great. Did I wake like this because I'd just had five hours' peaceful sleep?"

*Doctor:* "Only partly, but mostly because you are understanding more and recovering. However, recovery will still take time, and tomorrow morning may not be as peaceful.

You must accept this with good grace. If you had to go into a crisis at work tomorrow, your head would probably feel dull again, and the old iron band would grip and you'd think, 'That three weeks' holiday hasn't done any good at all!'" (He'd just had three weeks' holiday.) "Don't despair if this happens. Simply accept that more time must pass. That's all. The holiday has done its work. You can't estimate the amount of good it's done. The good is there. When you go back to the familiar scenes of suffering, the suffering will not seem quite as close as it was before you went away. Even that short respite from suffering will allow you to look *down* upon it, to understand and accept it with a little less agitation and despair.

"Understanding and willing acceptance are still the same old magic you must use now. Don't expect too much and so add disappointment to the picture. Just give it time.

"You will still have to think as slowly as your tired mind allows. Try not to become impatient or angry with yourself. Think, 'All right! All right! I'll go through with this. I'll take it slowly and quietly. I'm not going to thrash my battery.' Tread water without adding disappointment and despair."

*Patient:* "If I'm given some bad news when I go back, how will I cope with that?"

*Doctor:* "Let the first shock pass. Don't act on the moment's reaction. Let the reaction spend itself. Let your body do what it wants to and don't fight to try to save yourself from it. Let the reaction come. Accept it. You will find, that after you go through the initial shock, as your body calms down, you will think of ways to cope."

*Patient:* "I know I blow things up out of proportion; my wife says, 'How can you be so stupid!' I say, 'I don't know. I wish I did!' For a long time I couldn't bring myself to accept that I, so confident, had lost myself. Now I can accept it."

*Doctor:* "And also being a man of action, you want to do something about it quick! It is difficult for you to accept

that you get better quicker by doing nothing active about
it. Actually, although you appear to do nothing, you are
doing something very positive and very difficult: you are
accepting the state you are in. This is tremendous. It has
taken you months, hasn't it, to understand? You wanted a
switch to turn off the suffering quickly. You all search for
an outside switch—a new tablet, a new doctor."
*Patient:* "It's the hardest part for me to master, but it's
beginning to come. I don't know what to do about the
Valium. Should I start cutting down now?"
*Doctor:* "Not yet. I don't want you complicating recovery
by having withdrawal symptoms at this stage. And when
you decide to stop taking them, don't do it suddenly.
Anyhow, I'll help you with that." (I had not prescribed the
Valium.)

"You will know you are getting better as you begin to
handle stress without so much reaction. Certainly some
stress will come at work, but you will find you can sail
through it. In other words, your nerves will have regained
some of their normal insulation—they will not be so easily
aroused."

**Final interview with the same patient.** *Patient:* "I'm
still afraid to think, 'Look, you're on top of the world!'
even though I feel like it."
*Doctor:* "You can think of it, providing you're prepared to
be afraid of thinking it! What does it matter if you are
afraid to think it? That kind of fear is all part of getting
better. Up one minute and down the next! Up and down!
What the heck! Why worry about the downs? They pass.
When you can accept tomorrow as it comes, you are
recovering all the time. Acceptance that tomorrow may
not be so good alone relieves some tension. Acceptance
means that you are no longer thinking, 'This is wonderful,
but I wonder what I'll be like tomorrow!'"
*Patient:* "What came over me on my holiday? Why did I
slip back, Doctor? Why did I slip right back when I was
doing so well? After that second week when I started to go

to pieces, you said on the telephone for me to keep occupied normally: to take drives, have fun, lead the kind of life I would normally lead on such a holiday. I did and I started to pick up and then, after one bad night, I started to worry again because I wanted to be so much better by the end of the three weeks when I knew I had to go home and face work again. So I panicked. After two weeks when I thought I was getting better, down I went."

*Doctor:* "You did it to yourself, you know, by putting a time limit on getting better. You gave yourself that constant tension; can you see that?"

*Patient:* "Yes and I was so depressed by the setback. By the third week I was really down, worse than when I first arrived."

*Doctor:* "You sought to relieve stress, and yet in your ignorance you created it with too much anxious watching, expectation. You did not let time pass, you know."

*Patient:* "My biggest problem is that the sickness I've had over the last couple of years has been because of a tremendous amount of pressure—strain and worry with the business. I felt it as a persistent pounding the minute I walked into the office. There were only very short times for enjoyment and rest; I was so hassled."

*Doctor:* "Need you go back to that pace?"

*Patient:* "No, I've got it running now. I'd close it all up before I'd go back to that! I'm not going to run away from it, but I'm going to use my brains now; I'm going to delegate more. I know now that other people can do the job as well as I can. I used to lie in bed and think about the problems until three in the morning and the only way I could get relief was to take alcohol. I think I've done a pretty good job these last twelve months getting out of that one."

*Doctor:* "You've got more out of today than on any previous visit. I think you have the hang of it now."

*Patient:* "I think I have, if for only one reason. I've always thought of an interval ahead like, 'Another month!' Then with holidays coming up, I'd think, 'By the end of the holiday I'll be okay!' Now I've come down to realize the truth. I went to Honolulu for three weeks and that didn't cure me. I went to Miami for two weeks and that didn't cure. I went to Sydney for two weeks, and that didn't cure me either. Now I know I can't say I'll be cured by a special time. I'm going back to the farm for the rest of the holiday and I hope I'll be a bit better, but I don't expect to be *that* much better, and I'm ready to accept even that."

*Doctor:* "You've got the right idea at last. That's what I mean when I say, 'Let more time pass.' Time is all yours, so be prepared to take it."

*Patient:* "But I'm the sort of person, makeup-wise, who can't accept humiliation. This is why I'm successful in business. I don't accept anything as impossible. I couldn't accept that I, of all people, could get into this state. I probably wouldn't be like this if I'd been a different kind of person. I guess I just couldn't accept."

*Doctor:* "In the beginning I warned you that you probably wouldn't go back recovered and that you had to accept that. You had to learn that recovery takes its own time and you have to give that to it. It's the old four concepts: face, accept, float, and let time pass. Every time you have a setback you should say, 'Okay, more time must pass.' When you go home, at first you may feel good, at ease, and yet when you get into the office where you expect to still feel better, you may suddenly feel like hell. So what? That particular moment of hell is going to pass. Push the carrot at the end of the stick a little further away and pack that moment, that day, behind you."

*Patient:* "But the mornings are still pretty bad."

*Doctor:* "So what? They are likely to be bad for some time yet. You've been under tension for a long time. It may still be a gigantic effort to drag your body out of bed in the mornings for a few months yet."

*Patient:* "I drink a lot of coffee and smoke a lot. Does that help to cause the tiredness?"

*Doctor:* "Perhaps a little, but you are young and vital. By this I don't mean that when you are better you should continue drinking a lot of coffee and smoking. I mean that any harm it could do now is as nothing compared with what you do to yourself with your anxiety and fear. Be sure to eat enough nourishing food and leave the rest to time.

"You have to accept that you bashed your nervous system and that it will extract its revenge for a while. You are your nervous system, you know, and when it records your emotions in an exaggerated way and quickly, you feel as if your foundation has been shaken. And that's hard to understand, hard to cope with. You're flabbergasted by what you have done to yourself. It's difficult to live for one hour, let alone days, weeks, with a body that can respond so sensitively, even to a passing breeze. You feel, 'This is crazy! I must be going mad!' But you aren't. Your nerves are just overdoing their job, too eager to oblige."

*Patient:* "When that young girl asked me to play tennis on holiday, I thought, 'I'll never be able to handle it!' And the minute I worried about it I felt weak and I went down, down, down and stopped playing. And yet in the afternoon, I went water-skiing and came back and felt so good. But the next morning I was down again. And yet in the afternoon, I played two hours' table tennis. The next day, I couldn't even hold a paddle! Oh, God! It's confusing!"

*Doctor:* "When you felt so good skiing and playing table tennis you thought, 'This is it! I've made it!' But you hadn't you know. Instead you should have thought: 'Okay, this is good! I'm really enjoying this! What the heck if I feel tired tomorrow. Eventually I'll feel good all the time!'"

*Patient:* "I really do see at last, doctor. I know where I went wrong."

This man is fully recovered.

## SECOND PATIENT

TREMBLING HANDS. *Doctor:* "If I had a magic wand, what would you like me to waft away?"

*Patient:* "The strange feelings I get when I'm handling a cup of tea or a drinking glass. It's when I'm in certain situations; for instance, if I were here on business and you offered me a drink of tea, it would be okay if you offered it in a mug. If it were a flimsy kind of cup, I'd probably use my left hand to pick it up. My right hand would be shaking. That sort of maneuver can get carried to an extreme in an emergency.

"If I can rationalize the situation, I can manage. I spend my life watching myself to see that I don't land in too many predicaments. There are dozens of ways you can do a Houdini on yourself and slip out of an embarrassing situation without the obsession being obvious to others."

*Doctor:* "The basis of your fear is not of the actual shaking but of making a fool of yourself before other people. If it were the fear of shaking, or fear of the episode that originally caused the shaking (which we've just been discussing), your hand would shake whether you were in company or not."

*Patient:* "You're right. It's fear of what people will think."

*Doctor:* "There is only one way to cure it permanently. I'll tell you first about a girl who came to me with trembling hands. She'd saved for a long time for a trip to England. She'd been there only a month, when she had a severe shock and her hands began to tremble. She went to many doctors, including neurologists. In her words, she'd been 'all over the place,' but nothing stopped the shaking. Her money had run out, and since it is not easy to get a job, especially with shaking hands, she returned to Australia.

"I said to her, 'You've gone about curing yourself the wrong way by trying to stop your hands from shaking. I want you to let them shake. Don't try to control them. You have to decide what is the most important: letting them shake in front of people and living a normal life or avoiding people because of trembling hands. Your hands don't tremble when you are alone. It's being with people that causes the tension. And that means you are frightened *that they will tremble*! She said she was prepared to try letting them tremble. I added that she must be prepared for this even if drinking tea with the queen. She said that that wouldn't be easy because she was afraid she would spill her tea."

*Patient:* "So am I! That's just it!"

*Doctor:* "I know. So I told her to keep the saucer under the cup while she practiced. She came back a week later, and the shakes had gone. She said, 'If only one of those doctors in London had told me that, I could still be there!'

"You see, by tensely trying to control the trembling that was caused by tension, she had simply brought more tension, and this is exactly what you are doing. Sometimes you avoid the tension by bluffing yourself—you know, the idea of drinking from a mug and not a cup. But you can't always use a mug."

*Patient:* "Are you telling me that I must be prepared to spill the tea?"

*Doctor:* "Yes. Admit to any onlooker that your hands would probably shake and then be prepared to drink from any kind of container. It's more important for you to lose fear of what others may think than it is for you to go on trying to hide your fear by making excuses, or using a mug instead of a cup."

*Patient:* "Must I say straight out that my hands may shake?"

*Doctor:* "Yes."

*Patient:* "What if it is a glass with no saucer, or worse still, if it's wine!"

*Doctor:* "Put your handkerchief underneath; use anything."

*Patient:* "Even in a restaurant?"

*Doctor:* "Of course, because that's where you're most frightened."

*Patient:* "Don't I know it! When they give you such a little coffee cup at the end of the meal. It's ironic. One place will turn the shakes on and another won't!"

*Doctor:* "I want you to be prepared to have them turned on, so that eventually it won't matter what the place is like."

*Patient:* "I understand. I have a sort of routine of security now. I go to a place where I know the girls will bring the coffee over to me and I won't have to pick it up."

*Doctor:* "I want you to be free of all that. And the only way you can do this is to let your hand shake; *let it tremble*. By degrees, if you do this, you will become so used to the trembling that it won't worry you any more. As humans we adapt well, and I want you to adapt to having a trembling hand. You haven't adapted so far; you've been running away, trying to cover up. You will find it more difficult to accept when you're tired."

*Patient:* "I feel I'm ready to accept while I'm here with you, but being able to do it willingly, as you say, when the time comes and someone's watching me—I don't know. At least I'll try."

*Doctor:* "You may not be successful on the first attempt, but if you persevere, I assure you, the shaking will gradually not matter. Especially when you finally feel, deep within yourself, that your *freedom from the fear of it* is more important than *it*."

## THIRD PATIENT

THIS IS A CRAZY BUSINESS. *Patient:* "At the level of recovery I reached, with the help of an occasional tranquilizer, I was able to carry on in quite an important position for 10 years after I first saw you. Then I thought, 'I've handled this all right, so now I'll retire.'

"I found that the reason I had been able to cope was that although I felt lousy nearly every morning and fought my way to work, the moment I became engrossed in work—especially if it was a research project—I felt okay. But sometimes, as soon as I became aware of feeling better, I almost immediately felt awful again. But this is the way it goes, isn't it, doctor? It's an on-and-off affair."

*Doctor:* "Yes. Suddenly finding yourself normal acts like a shock, so back come the anxiety and symptoms. You must learn to treat the sudden awareness of normality as one of those flash moments I have taught you to pass through. Recovery brings many flash moments that shock."

*Patient:* "I can remember right back in my childhood, I had the same experiences. Why was it that when I could play an excellent game of football on important occasions, 10 minutes after playing well, I'd feel suddenly so tired I hardly had the energy to lift one foot off the ground? It was the same when I was going to school. I used to ride 20 miles on horseback each day. Many times I've set out in the morning, most likely in tears, not knowing how I'd face the day and yet, after I settled at school, I'd do a good day's work. I've often wondered, are you born with a predisposition to this sort of thing?"

*Doctor:* "Some can't summon energy as quickly as others. I remember when I was a student at the university, one senior girl once said to me at breakfast, 'I can't bear to look at you, Weekes! It's indecent to be so energetic so early in the morning!' And yet by night she was firing on all cylinders and I could hardly keep my eyes open. It could be a question of one's particular metabolic rhythm. With you I suspect that the cause was, still is, emotional. You see, you're in your sixties now and I doubt if you would have ever reached that age if the cause had been organic. No, I think with you, it has always been emotional."

*Patient:* "I think you're right. When my mother's sister was in the hospital for a month and I had to visit her every day, I felt better than I had for years. I thought, 'This is a crazy business!' I could only figure that I was so busy concentrating on her that I forgot about myself."

*Doctor:* "Our thoughts and emotions can be so closely tied that when we establish a pattern of anxious thought, emotional reaction can be triggered so quickly that it seems almost reflexive. Your morning suffering is very much like this; you think, from habit, about feeling tired and then of course, out of habit, you feel tired. If there was something that demanded immediate action, you wouldn't have time to feel fatigued. When you were

140

young, you had only to feel tired on several similar occasions to remember and associate fatigue with that kind of occasion. You established a habit."

*Patient:* "I can understand that."

*Doctor:* "I remember after a major operation, when I had to return to work after a few weeks and cope with an office full of patients, I would look up the hill I had to climb in the morning and think, 'I'll never make it!' Yet later in the day, after walking a few miles between my desk and the examination table, I felt stronger. If I had spent the day lying about at home thinking about how weak I was, I doubt if I would have recovered so quickly."

*Patient:* "It's as I said, with the help of your philosophy and a few tranquilizers occasionally, I got through the last years of my active life. After I retired I was real well for a while. Then I found I was running out of things to do. I still had apprehension about doing certain jobs, and when you retire there is a special apprehension, a second lot of challenges to meet!"

*Doctor:* "When you retire you lose the stimulation of company. There may be too much time to fill in, trying to find jobs, too much time to think about yourself and how you feel."

*Patient:* "Making myself do what I know I have to do is the hurdle I have to get over. For example, yesterday I was in this lousy state in the morning thinking, 'I've got to play in that wretched game against Saint Luke's.' I thought, 'I can't do this!' And then the little voice said, 'Well, you've just got to do it! You've just got to have a go, mate!' And sure enough I'd find when I'd get up there and play, it would be okay and when the game's all over, I'd think, 'I've been playing this damn match for four hours and I'm feeling good! I should feel exhausted!'"

*Doctor:* "You know why, of course? During those four hours your mind was on the bowls and not on how you felt. Also, it didn't matter to you how you felt; you knew you had to play on. Not-mattering was the key, as well as thinking of things outside yourself."

*Patient:* "There are always odd jobs to cope with, and Jerry, my eldest son, usually rings me the night before if I'm going down to help him and says, 'Now listen Dad, this is what you've got to bring,' and he gives me a list, and then he says, 'Right. Have you got it all down?' He's a real wag, that one.

"So we set out to go down and I think, 'Holy mackerel! I've got to drive down there and it will be a couple of hours going down! That'll be hell!' But by the time I get to the Harbour Bridge, I've forgotten about worrying and I'm concentrating on driving."

*Doctor:* "There is so much habit in your suffering. When you think about a long drive, you imagine doing the whole two hours in one moment of contemplation. Whereas once you start, you do it minute by minute and that's so much easier, especially when your attention is diverted while you drive. When you are sitting contemplating, you condense the moments into one big obstacle, almost like a concrete wall that has to be got through before you can reach your destination. Action helps tremendously. As I always say, contemplation is the killer. With contemplation you see the whole drive as a very tiring operation and you imagine yourself doing it—the entire drive—during those moments when you are just thinking about it. No wonder it seems tiring!"

## FOURTH PATIENT

RECURRING SYMPTOMS. *Patient:* "It's difficult to believe that the symptoms can recur after weeks of peace."
*Doctor:* "Yes, and they may not come back gently either, even though you are recovering. The contrast between the good you've been feeling and how bad you can suddenly feel seems incredible."
*Patient:* "I felt marvelous."
*Doctor:* "It is difficult for you to understand, and yet the explanation is simple. Recovery from nervous illness is

usually fairly slow. You can't quickly forget what you've been through. It's rather like losing through death someone you loved; after a while you can go for weeks without too much suffering, and then suddenly the unexpected sight of something belonging to them recalls memories and desolation sweeps again."

*Patient:* "That's right. I've had a nasty few days and feel I'll never get better. Desolation? I'll say!"

*Doctor:* "It's difficult, isn't it, to realize that you are going through a phase of recovery. A strange phase that keeps repeating itself. It's difficult to realize that what will liberate you is simply release from tension through understanding. When you fully understand, it is as if a physical weight is lifted from your chest. You feel freer. Can even think more flexibly."

*Patient:* "The most frightening aspect for me is that although there is no reason that I can see, a setback seems to pounce with the force of an elephant. Then I start to wonder, 'Am I thinking straight?' Driving over here this afternoon, I was even a bit frightened again, and I realized that my thoughts were coming just that fraction slower and this made me apprehensive. Things even looked a little strange."

*Doctor:* "You suddenly felt mentally tired in that car. If we were to say that when mentally fresh we function at about 100 percent of normal, I'd say that you are now functioning at about 75 percent and that any extra strain, such as driving the car in traffic, although little, can be enough to bring back the symptoms of mental fatigue. Your present reserve of mental energy is low. You may have occasional flashes of feeling 100 percent, perhaps after a rest or sleep, and these flashes of feeling normal can be very confusing."

*Patient:* "Realizing it is only fatigue helps enormously, especially hearing you say it. Fatigue seems to be the key."

*Doctor:* "Since your extreme nervous exhaustion, you haven't had a long enough experience of feeling well. You haven't experienced enough to be sure that a setback will always pass."

*Patient:* "I have no certainty at all, only your word."

*Doctor:* "That's why I say, 'Let more time pass.'"

*Patient:* "When I'm working, keeping my train of thought going is very difficult. It's frightening. Sometimes I feel half-witted."

*Doctor:* "Don't be afraid of feeling like that. How you feel at that moment is temporary although embarrassing. Remember it is only temporary, and float on. Loosen and accept. Go on quietly, half-witted or not."

*Patient:* "Yes and while I am fatigued and sensitized, all the terrible, frightening things going on in the world seem so much more frightening!"

*Doctor:* "We're all concerned about that, but a sensitized person can feel the concern physically. You know, even announcers make the news seem worse when they hand it out in a doomsday voice. It's a wonder we're not all crazy."

*Patient:* "But I shouldn't be frightened like this. It's ridiculous."

*Doctor:* "In your present state you are submerged by circumstances. Your control fluctuates; for example, if you have a problem, one day you can see it in perspective—you're on top of it, looking down on it—but the next day, especially if you are tired, it seems on top of you.

"Some days you can think, 'Oh yes, I will be able to cope with that!' while the next day you are sure you haven't a hope of coping. You feel as if you have a block in your mind. However, you do cope in spite of the block."

*Patient:* "Morning is my worst time. My mind wanders round and round. It's the same every morning. I know I have to get myself used to it. I have to accept that. The thoughts aren't even logical. They come in streams that run in every direction. Again I am apprehensive about recovering."

*Doctor:* "As I said, you have no firm foundation for peace yet, no platform from which you can look down on your thoughts. At the moment you are carried away by them like a drowning man in a riptide. Those early morning hours are very difficult to get through, especially when you have to listen to morning sounds you've been hearing for weeks: familiar sounds that bring back the memory of other moments of acute suffering. They seem to drag you back, make you feel you've made no progress. You know? . . . The dog that starts barking at the same time each morning. Wouldn't you like to shoot it sometimes?"

*Patient:* "Fortunately we live in a very peaceful spot. I've learned now that the thing to do is to get up and get a drink of something. A glass of hot milk."

*Doctor:* "Doing something familiar makes you feel more normal, more real—it breaks the spell."

*Patient:* "Yes, but the milk also does seem to settle me."

*Doctor:* "There's supposed to be a chemical in milk that helps sleep. However, just going out into a brighter light, being with familiar things helps most, I think. They help you to get strange rambling thoughts into perspective. You can see that they are rambling, that the strangeness is you, going through a special phase in your illness; that it is simply born from the way you are feeling at this moment. Don't take any strangeness too seriously at this stage."

## LATER TALK WITH THE SAME PATIENT

HALF-BAKED—NOT WITH IT. *Doctor:* "When you are emerging from nervous illness, feeling good is such a contrast to the way you have so often felt in the past that the contrast can seem almost like a mild shock. It's the quickness of the body's reaction to the sudden realization of how close suffering is that unbalances. One minute you feel good, the next apprehensive again. You have to learn that such flash moments are inevitable during recovery and that you have to pass through them again and again. I call going through these flashes being back in the spin-dryer."

*Patient:* "Today I've been flicking off the fear quite well, but I had to do it every little while. One flick doesn't do the job!"

145

*Doctor:* "Sometimes it seems as if your mind has tentacles that keep clutching and bringing you back to it. You can't understand how you will ever escape them, will ever stop reverting to thinking about yourself. A young man described this well. He said that one night when he was desperately caught in this trap, a neighbor called and stood talking in the door, swinging a lantern. The swinging lantern caught his attention, and momentarily he forgot to think inwardly. Suddenly he understood that he could lose this habit of inward thinking just as he could lose any other habit. He could see that it was only a habit. He also saw that it did not matter what he thought; that he could just as well think, 'Tick!' as think about himself. He also saw that if he were unafraid of it, any outside interest could claim his attention and the habit itself would be lost. He felt suddenly elated. He had found the way through! He thought, 'Flick on! What the heck!' Can you understand this?" (Also discussed on p. 124.)

*Patient:* "Yes. You mean that when the thoughts flick inward all day, I have to let them flick and know that gradually, as I do this, I will become more interested in doing other things, and the habit will go because it won't worry me?"

*Doctor:* "Yes. Its presence won't matter any more."

*Patient:* "That won't be easy to do."

*Doctor:* "It's the *only* way."

*Patient:* "I get so tired, I can't help sometimes wishing it all to hell!"

*Doctor:* "Wish that as often as you like, but at the same time understand that it's only memory, habit, and fear working together to form this habit. There is no 'it' doing this to you; there's just that wretched trio. It's as if your thoughts are caught and made to run in one track. When they've been in that track all day, naturally you despair. But beneath the despair, remember it's only habit, memory, and tension from fear and fatigue. However, losing this habit is different from losing other habits. You can't think, 'I'll stop!' and then stop (for instance, like stopping smoking). You must let it come and learn to make it part of your ordinary thinking and not think of it as forbidden territory— something you must not think.'"

*Patient:* "When I talk to you I understand and feel courage and am sure I will be able to do it. But as well as losing that habit, what worries me is the feeling of being half-baked, not 'with it.'"

*Doctor:* "That's mental fatigue. This is the devil, isn't it? And you're going through a lot of it because of your constant anxiety about it and the kind of brain work you do. Don't think, 'I've got to find a way out of all this!' You haven't. Your body, your mind, will find a way if you simply remember acceptance. Accept and let your body and mind do the rest. There is no mystery. Accept whatever happens at the moment, even though you may think it's driving you crazy."

*Patient:* "That's just what's been making me so fearful— the thought that I'm going mad!"

*Doctor:* "And when fearful, you become especially tense and that's when ideas really stick, and that's when you think you're going mad. You've tried to live with so much, to conquer so much."

*Patient:* "Two weeks ago I was free! What's happened now to take me back into it all again?"

*Doctor:* "Don't look back. You must look forward. You are still very vulnerable to repeats of 'it'; please accept that. But, of course, then comes that strange experience that when you do relax and are free, you think, 'I hope I don't have to go back into that again!' You tense at this very thought, and, of course, you can then be so easily drawn into thinking inwardly once more. But that's part of getting better. Take the whole lot and think, 'What will be will be!' Don't try to direct. Submit. Hang the lot! And take what comes!'"

*Patient:* "I'm doing that 95 percent of the time, but I slip back on the other 5 percent."

*Doctor:* "You think you've slipped back, but all you've done is to slip once more into the wrong groove. Thoughts

quickly become grooved. Your thoughts repeat themselves like a needle stuck in the groove of a record. You think there is no way out. There is. Accept the groove always as part of your ordinary thinking. *Stay in the groove willingly.*"
*Patient:* "Here we go again!"

He went very well indeed.

# 7

# Talk Given at National Phobia Conference

*Talk given as guest speaker at the Fourth National Phobia Conference sponsored by the Phobia Society of America and Phobia Clinic, White Plains Hospital Medical Center, New York, 7 May 1983*

As we all know, there are many different ways of treating nervous illness. I am speaking now of anxiety states with, or without, obsessions, phobias.

I recently read a book in which the author described most of the common methods of treatment of nervous illness used today. While they seemed different, they each claimed a good record of success. Whatever the treatment, in my opinion, success will depend on the sufferer's attitude to it.

If he is convinced that it will help him, the chances are it will; you know the saying "Nothing is but thinking makes it so." However, in my opinion, a treatment based mainly on belief in it is in danger of working only temporarily. While the person treated continues to believe that it will work, he's probably safe; but let him begin to doubt, and he's in for trouble. Let him begin to doubt any outside crutch on which he depends, and he's in danger.

For recovery, the sufferer must have, deep within himself, a special voice that says during any setback or dark moment, "It's all right; you've been here before. You know the way out. You can do it again. It works, you know it works!" That voice speaks with authority and brings comfort only when it has been earned by the sufferer himself, and it can be earned only by making the symptoms and experiences that torture *no longer matter*. NO-LONGER-MATTERING IS THE KEY. It is not a question of some method of treatment spiriting misery away, anesthetizing it. It is a question of the symptoms, the experiences, no-longer-mattering.

The necessity for the sufferer himself to earn the inner voice of assurance does not exclude outside help—for example, by giving understanding and direction and if possible by alleviating difficult, stressful circumstances.

The person alone all day with no program of recovery to follow, no special interesting work to do, who has somehow to fill each hour (the exhausted housewife struggling to cope with the work, perhaps with a couple of children dragging at her skirt), the person who thinks himself too ill and weary to work, and who is ill and weary with adrenal glands depleted by too intense and too frequent stress—what a mountain such people have to climb to earn that inner voice, especially if panic and other symptoms come by merely thinking about them.

These people's minds are all geared ready to thwart, ready at every turn to put up a barricade. The mind will remember and remind, mock, tantalize, never leaving the body alone. It will twist, turn, spiral, cavort—always turning inward, inward, inward, clinging with tentacles of glue.

And yet all through this turmoil, the right comforting voice is there to be discovered. However, the sufferer needs to be shown how to make this discovery, how to make his torture no longer matter. It is not enough to simply have it subdued. Balance must be struck between the sufferer doing the work by himself and being helped. So the question is: What outside help should be given? First, let us consider tranquilization.

A while ago, I read in a London newspaper an article by a journalist who said she had been agoraphobic for many years but could now go anywhere simply by taking a certain tablet three times a day. She gave the name of the pill, said she'd tried all the others and that none had worked as well as this one.

"And now," said she, "all I have to do is come off that little pill!" That's all she had to do—simply come off that pill. Only that! She had no idea that she was announcing that she had left her future in the hands of chance. She had left it to chance, because so much would depend on what she thought on the very day when she first went without her pills. I notice she wrote the article first.

If, on that special day, she thought, "Well, all is well . . . I can go anywhere now. I don't need the pill. The pill's not important any longer; so I can forget about it!"—if she thought that way and did forget about the pill, all could be well—temporarily. I say temporarily, because if stress—similar to the stress that had originally brought her symptoms—returned, or if she simply thought of panic and panicked (particularly in some awkward situation), I wonder how long it would be before she reached for a pill? I don't really wonder; I know. It wouldn't be very long. And when she succumbed, how long before her inner voice said, "You'll probably always need that pill, you know!" And that would be her master's voice speaking. The pill would be the master now.

And the voice could go on and say, "And what will you do if it doesn't work this time! What will you do then?" I leave you to use your imagination about that one. (Also discussed on p. 23.)

There is another kind of outside help: the kind used by quite a few self-help groups that teach members to go as far as they can without panicking and then if they feel panic, to come back and try again another day, until they can do that particular journey comfortably—without panicking.

But what will the inner voice say if, having got used

to all those places, one day, when out, a member of that group—perhaps tired, perhaps sensitized by some worry, or perhaps simply remembering how he used to panic— what if he panics again? What does his little voice say then? It has a heyday.

One man in Canada belonged to a group of agoraphobic people who worked this way. He felt so far recovered that he was able to travel into the United States and managed very well. I believe he went as far as Las Vegas and did not panic.

The day after he returned home he went down to the bank to draw some money. The same old bank, the same teller with the thick-lensed glasses, even the same bankbook with the torn corner, and as he handed the bankbook to the teller he stood on the exact spot where he had so often panicked before. Of course, memory smote, and on came panic and *it was a smasher!* It beat all records, because with it came anguish and despair—above all, despair. From then on, he wasn't even back in square one; he was back in square minus-one. And his inner voice shouted, "What are you going to do now? If, after all those months of getting-used-to, after all those weeks of success- ful traveling in the United States, if after all that, you can't even go to your bank without panicking, what *are* you going to do now?" (Also discussed on p. 21.)

Then there is the person who gets help from a special doctor and who uses the doctor as a more or less perma- nent crutch. What happens if that doctor leaves the dis- trict, and the sufferer has to depend on himself? (He doesn't like the other doctors in the town much, and they're not too keen on him.) What does his inner voice say? Well, it says the same old, "What are you going to do now? You're really lost this time, brother!"

That doctor had been very kind and thoughtful, but he had been no real help. He'd been a crutch for too long.

There is only one way to cure, and that is for the therapist to help his patient develop an inner voice that says in a crisis, "Go on, through. You've done it before. It works. You know it works. On, through!" An inner voice that is followed by a feeling of inner strength. *A real physical feeling*. Almost as if a piece of iron rod takes the place of quivering jelly.

Some of you are, I know, skeptical of my using the word *cure*, especially if I had said permanent cure. I am aware that many therapists believe there is no permanent cure for nervous illness. When I was on radio some years ago in New York with a physician and a psychiatrist, the psychiatrist corrected me when I used the word *cure* and said, "You mean remission, don't you, Dr. Weekes? We never speak of curing nervous illness!" I told her that I had cured far too many nervously ill people to be afraid to use the word.

I suppose that were we to say that if a person saw a murder committed before his eyes, there would be no hope of his completely forgetting it, we would be right. I think that perhaps that is what some therapists mean when they say nervous illness cannot be cured, only relieved. They believe that memory will always return and that the nerves of a once nervously ill person may respond to memory with such intensity because of their past experience, that the poor devil is doomed. I think maybe that's what they mean. Also, I suspect that some therapists who deny cure of nervous illness may think, "Once a weakling, always a weakling." Maybe.

Of course, memory is always capable of recalling nervous symptoms, and what a heyday an anxious inner voice has then. It says, "It's all back again! Every lock, stock, and barrel. Every member of the family! We're all here. What are you going to do now? You'll never recover now, you know!" What power the wrong voice holds. But if the right earned voice is there it will come to the rescue and say, "You've been here before, you know the way!" Then, in spite of being possibly shocked and temporarily thrown off balance, the owner of that inner voice does know what to do and gradually does it.

And that's what I mean by cure: having the right

inner voice to support and lead through setbacks, through
flash moments of despair, through bewilderment. That is
cure. I don't mean that the once nervously ill person will
always be at peace, will not have setbacks. Of course he
may; surely he's entitled to be human. I mean that for a
person to be cured, he must be able to take setbacks as
they come (and they may come unexpectedly 30 years or
more after the original illness), must take the setback
directed by an inner voice that is the real tranquilizer.
This is my meaning of cure.

And after each setback that inner voice is strengthened,
and what is more, each setback successfully navigated by
that voice reinforces confidence and self-esteem. Can you
see how important, almost essential, setbacks are when
the right inner voice is being developed to be the guide?

I supposed it's a lucky person who goes through life
without being nervously ill. But I wonder. A person who
has been nervously ill has widened his understanding, his
power to appreciate, to feel compassion, even to enjoy.

But of course he has to carry the scar of memory. You
know the saying "Where ignorance is bliss, 'tis folly to be
wise." But if the sufferer has developed the strong, right
inner voice, there is not so much folly for him in being
wise.

But without the right voice, all is left to chance, and
that's very chancy. Also, the person, who has been "cured"
(and I put "cured" in quotes) by chance, by luck, by some
outside crutch on which he continues to depend, can know
only the peace of ignorance and that's no peace at all. It is
only a temporary quietness. As long as his luck holds, he's
probably okay. But luck has a habit of changing. It's a fool
who trusts his life to luck, and we are talking about
people's lives.

So I believe, in the work I have done, I have tried to
show the patient how to develop the right inner voice.
The person who recovers using the four concepts that I
teach—facing, accepting, floating, and letting time pass—

has done so by *going through hell the right way* and so has developed that right inner voice.

But in doing so, he has to put his head on the block, has to put himself into stressful situations that he otherwise would have avoided. And that's where he often falters, even sometimes fails. However, I teach him to know that peace lies on the other side of panic, on the other side of failure, never on this side.

There is a clinic in Toronto, Canada, specializing in treating nervous illness whose superintendent wrote to me and asked permission to use phrases from one of my books. He said he had these printed on ballpoint pens which he gave to patients. One of the phrases chosen was: "Recovery lies in the places and experiences you fear." And that, in my opinion, is exactly right. I teach my patients never to be put off by the places and experiences they fear. These are their salvation.

The person who ventures into these places and experiences will of course sensitize himself more than if he avoided them; so I come again to the question of tranquilization.

For some people I prescribe temporary tranquilization, but, of course, I tailor the dose to the person. I always bear in mind that to earn the right kind of inner voice, the sufferer must go through his experiences acutely enough to learn that facing, accepting, and floating do the real work. He would never know this if he were continuously tranquilized. As I say, the question of tranquilization is a delicate one and must be tailored to the individual.

There are people who can, and prefer to, go through the greatest hell without tranquilizers; however, the majority want, and need, to be helped with tranquilizers during the most severe stages of their illness.

Nervous illness is so very tiring. There is not only muscular, emotional, and mental fatigue, there is also a kind of fatigue of the spirit, when the will to survive falters. I have found that when people reach this stage, to sedate and let them sleep even for a few hours can make all the difference. It can refresh enough for them to find courage and strength to go on once more.

In my opinion, this is one of the main uses of tranquilizers—to relieve fatigue and also to take the sharp edge off suffering, when suffering becomes almost too great for a body to bear.

I say almost, because there are those who can and do bear it. However, we should never demand this unreasonably from our patients. As I say, tranquilization must be temporary and tailored to the individual.

So I leave you all with a suggestion: those of you treating nervous illness should find out what the inner voice of your patients is saying. In my opinion, when we think we have cured a patient but have not helped him earn the right inner voice, we have not cured at all, whatever method used.

If some of you suffer from nervous illness, find out what your inner voice is saying. Be honest about it. Face it. If it brings no reassurance, find a voice that does—by facing, accepting, floating, and letting time pass. And remember, when we learn to walk and live *with* fear, we eventually walk and live *without* fear.

# Index

# Index

Identity, lost, 79, 80
Illness, fear of, 112–13
Imagination, 96, 107; *see also* Thoughts
Imbalance, mental, 12
Indecision, 95, 106
Insanity, fear of, 9, 12, 16, 95, 123, 147
Insomnia, 52–54
Introspection, 14, 17, 18, 36, 47, 56, 68, 116, 124–26, 146, 150
and depression, 131
Irritation, 110–11

Joy, felt hysterically, 10, 11–12
of life, 51, 78

Labeling, 55
Lethargy, *see* Apathy, and Fatigue
Letting go, *see* Acceptance, and Floating
Letting time pass, 21, 33–37, 56, 74, 87, 97, 134–35, 154
Light, sensitivity to, 17–18, 98
Lightheadedness, 8, 39, 75, 94; *see also* Fainting, fear of
Loneliness, *see* Aloneness
Love, intensified, 11

Medical examinations, 110
Medication, *see* Tranquilization
Meditation, 105
Memory, 14, 34, 38–39, 47, 61, 73, 96, 100, 102, 146, 153–54
difficulty in remembering, 14, 51, 106
Mood, 24, 51–52, 81, 105, 128
Motivation, 18–19, 61
and group therapy, 119
Muscle, tension, 4–5, 38–39, 122–23
jerks, 8
weakness, 8; *see also* Fatigue, muscular
"Muzzy" head, 16–17, 94, 106, 115

Nausea, constant, 113–14
and medication, 114
Neighbors, 103–4
Nervous illness, definition, 2
and blood pressure, 110
duration of, 34–35, 68
and dying, 76–78
and eating, 113–14
and fatigue, 50, 66, 68–69, 75, 87, 96, 111
and fear of illness, 112–13
and job applications, 116–17
and life after recovery, 119–20
and living with relatives, 112
and old age, 60–62, 70–71
and socializing, 97, 119
Nervous system
involuntary, 7–8
parasympathetic, 7, 8
sympathetic, 7–8
voluntary, 7
Noise, sensitivity to, 10–11, 52–53
Nutrition, 62, 114
and hypoglycemia, 121–22

Obessions, 15–16, 42–44, 48, 58
and tension, 115–16
Occupation, 40, 50–51, 68, 70–71, 106–7, 150
and depression, 108
and applying for jobs, 116–17
Old age, 60–62, 70–71, 141

Panic, 22, 24, 27–28, 29, 44–46, 47, 55, 63–65, 78–81, 92
defused by acceptance, 85–87
and dying, 76–78
fear of, 27–28, 34, 44–45, 79–80, 92–93
first, 78–81
peak of, 93–94
super-panic, 44–46
"Paralysis", 30
Peace of mind, 25, 27, 41–42, 59, 61, 63, 113, 130–31; *see also* Acceptance

159

## ABOUT THE AUTHOR

In 1929, DR. CLAIRE WEEKES became the first woman to obtain the degree of Doctor of Science at the University of Sydney. She graduated with a degree in medicine from the University of Sydney in 1945, became a member of the Royal Australasian College of Physicians in 1955, and was elected fellow of the college in 1973. Following graduation, Dr. Weekes spent five years in general practice, was appointed honorary physician to the Rachel Forster Hospital in Sydney in 1956, and was named consultant physician in 1962—a position she holds today. Dr. Weekes is best known for her pioneering work in the study of nervous illness and anxiety. She has written two international bestsellers, *Hope and Help for Your Nerves* and *Peace from Nervous Suffering*, which together have sold more than 350,000 copies. She is also the author of *Simple, Effective Treatment of Agoraphobia*. In addition, Dr. Weekes has lectured at psychiatric hospitals in Britain and has spoken often on radio and television both in Britain and the United States.

# We Deliver!
## And So Do These Bestsellers.

| ☐ | 27724 | **TIME FLIES** by Bill Cosby | $4.95 |
| ☐ | 28467 | **LOVE AND MARRIAGE** by Bill Cosby | $4.95 |
| ☐ | 25660 | **THE PILL BOOK GUIDE TO SAFE DRUG USE** by Harold Silverman | $4.95 |
| ☐ | 27805 | **TALKING STRAIGHT** by Lee Iacocca w/Sonny Kleinfield | $5.50 |
| ☐ | 28057 | **THE LIVES OF JOHN LENNON** by Albert Goldman | $5.95 |
| ☐ | 27601 | **ULTIMATE EVIL** by Maury Terry | $5.95 |
| ☐ | 34388 | **800 COCAINE** by Mark S. Gold, M.D. | $3.95 |
| ☐ | 27826 | **FACTS ON DRUGS & ALCOHOL** by Mark S. Gold, M.D. | $3.95 |
| ☐ | 27926 | **GUINNESS BOOK OF WORLD RECORDS 1989** by Norris McWhirter | $4.95 |
| ☐ | 26401 | **MORE HOPE AND HELP FOR YOUR NERVES** by Claire Weekes | $4.50 |
| ☐ | 25962 | **PAUL HARVEY'S THE REST OF THE STORY** by Paul Aurandt | $3.95 |
| ☐ | 27976 | **BURNING BRIDGES: DIARY OF A MID-LIFE AFFAIR** by Inette Miller | $4.50 |
| ☐ | 28288 | **MOVIES ON TV &VIDEO CASSETTE 1990-1991** by Steve Scheuer | $5.95 |

Buy them at your local bookstore or use this page to order.

- - - - - - - - - - - - - - - - - - - - - - - -

**Bantam Books, Dept. NFB, 414 East Golf Road, Des Plaines, IL 60016**

Please send me the items I have checked above. I am enclosing $_____
(please add $2.00 to cover postage and handling). Send check or money
order, no cash or C.O.D.s please.

Mr/Ms _____

Address _____

City/State _____ Zip_____

NFB–3/90

Please allow four to six weeks for delivery.
Prices and availability subject to change without notice.

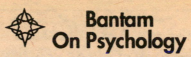

# Bantam
# On Psychology

- ☐ 28037 **MEN WHO HATE WOMEN & THE WOMEN WHO LOVE THEM** Dr. Susan Forward    $4.95
- ☐ 26401 **MORE HOPE AND HELP FOR YOUR NERVES** Claire Weekes    $4.50
- ☐ 27376 **HOPE AND HELP FOR YOUR NERVES** Claire Weekes    $4.50
- ☐ 26754 **PEACE FROM NERVOUS SUFFERING** Claire Weekes    $4.50
- ☐ 26005 **HOW TO BREAK YOUR ADDICTION TO A PERSON** Howard M. Halpern, Ph.D.    $4.95
- ☐ 27043 **THE POWER OF THE SUBCONSCIOUS MIND** Dr. J. Murphy    $4.50
- ☐ 34367 **TEACH ONLY LOVE** Gerald Jampolsky, M.D. (A Large Format Book)    $8.95
- ☐ 27087 **CUTTING LOOSE: An Adult Guide for Coming to Terms With Your Parents** Howard Halpern    $4.50
- ☐ 26390 **WHEN I SAY NO, I FEEL GUILTY** Manuel J. Smith    $5.50
- ☐ 28496 **SUPER JOY: IN LOVE WITH LIVING** Paul Pearsall    $5.50

## ALSO AVAILABLE ON AUDIO CASSETTE

- ☐ 45047 **BREAK YOUR ADDICTION TO A PERSON** Howard Halpern, Ph.D    $7.95
- ☐ 45080 **MEN WHO HATE WOMEN AND THE THE WOMEN WHO LOVE THEM** Susan Forward, Ph.D    $7.95
- ☐ 45121 **WHEN AM I GOING TO BE HAPPY? BREAK THE EMOTIONAL BAD HABITS THAT KEEP YOU FROM REACHING YOUR POTENTIAL** Penelope Russianoff, Ph.D    $8.95
- ☐ 45167 **TEACH ONLY LOVE** Gerald Jampolsky    $8.95
- ☐ 45130 **DEVELOP YOUR INTUITION: WOMEN**    $7.95

Buy them at your local bookstore or use this page for ordering.

**Bantam Books, Dept. ME, 414 East Golf Road, Des Plaines, IL 60016**

Please send me the items I have checked above. I am enclosing $_____ (please add $2.00 to cover postage and handling). Send check or money order, no cash or C.O.D.s please. (Tape offer good in USA only.)

Mr/Ms _____

Address _____

City/State _____ Zip _____

ME-2/90

Please allow four to six weeks for delivery.
Prices and availability subject to change without notice.

# INVEST IN THE POWERS OF YOUR MIND
# WITH SUBLIMINAL SELF-HELP TAPES
# FROM BANTAM AUDIO PUBLISHING

The Bantam Audio Self-Help series, produced by Audio Activation, combines sophisticated psychological techniques of behavior modification with subliminal stimulation to help you get what you want out of life.

## For Women

| | | | |
|---|---|---|---|
| ☐ | 45004 | SLIM FOREVER | $8.95 |
| ☐ | 45035 | STOP SMOKING FOREVER | $8.95 |
| ☐ | 45041 | STRESS-FREE FOREVER | $8.95 |
| ☐ | 45172 | DEVELOP A PERFECT MEMORY | $8.95 |
| ☐ | 45130 | DEVELOP YOUR INTUITION | $7.95 |
| ☐ | 45022 | POSITIVELY CHANGE YOUR LIFE | $8.95 |
| ☐ | 45106 | GET A GOOD NIGHT'S SLEEP...EVERY NIGHT | $7.95 |
| ☐ | 45094 | IMPROVE YOUR CONCENTRATION | $7.95 |
| ☐ | 45016 | PLAY TO WIN | $7.95 |
| ☐ | 45081 | YOU'RE IRRESISTIBLE | $7.95 |
| ☐ | 45112 | AWAKEN YOUR SENSUALITY | $7.95 |

## For Men

| | | | |
|---|---|---|---|
| ☐ | 45005 | SLIM FOREVER | $8.95 |
| ☐ | 45036 | STOP SMOKING FOREVER | $8.95 |
| ☐ | 45042 | STRESS-FREE FOREVER | $8.95 |
| ☐ | 45173 | DEVELOP A PERFECT MEMORY | $8.95 |
| ☐ | 45131 | DEVELOP YOUR INTUITION | $7.95 |
| ☐ | 45023 | POSITIVELY CHANGE YOUR LIFE | $8.95 |
| ☐ | 45107 | GET A GOOD NIGHT'S SLEEP...EVERY NIGHT | $7.95 |
| ☐ | 45095 | IMPROVE YOUR CONCENTRATION | $7.95 |
| ☐ | 45017 | PLAY TO WIN | $7.95 |
| ☐ | 45082 | YOU'RE IRRESISTIBLE | $7.95 |
| ☐ | 45113 | AWAKEN YOUR SENSUALITY | $7.95 |

Look for them at your local bookstore or use this handy page for ordering:

Bantam Books, Dept. BAP4, 414 East Golf Road, Des Plaines, IL 60016

Please send me ____ copies of the tapes the items I have checked. I am enclosing $_____ (please add $2.00 to cover postage and handling). Send check or money order, no cash or C.O.D.s please.

Mr/Ms _____

Address _____

City/State _____ Zip_____

BAP4—11/89

Please allow four to six weeks for delivery.
Prices and availability subject to change without notice.

# Special Offer
# Buy a Bantam Book
## *for only 50¢.*

*Now you can have Bantam's catalog filled with hundreds of titles plus take advantage of our unique and exciting bonus book offer. A special offer which gives you the opportunity to purchase a Bantam book for only 50¢. Here's how!*

*By ordering any five books at the regular price per order, you can also choose any other single book listed (up to a $5.95 value) for just 50¢. Some restrictions do apply, but for further details why not send for Bantam's catalog of titles today!*

*Just send us your name and address and we will send you a catalog!*

BANTAM BOOKS, INC.
P.O. Box 1006, South Holland, Ill. 60473

Mr./Mrs./Ms. _____
(please print)

Address _____

City _____ State _____ Zip _____

FC(A)-11/89

Please allow four to six weeks for delivery.

# By the year 2000, 2 out of 3 Americans could be illiterate.

It's true.

Today, 75 million adults… about one American in three, can't read adequately. And by the year 2000, U.S. News & World Report envisions an America with a literacy rate of only 30%.

Before that America comes to be, you can stop it… by joining the fight against illiteracy today.

Call the Coalition for Literacy at toll-free **1-800-228-8813** and volunteer.

## Volunteer Against Illiteracy. The only degree you need is a degree of caring.

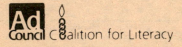

Ad Council  Coalition for Literacy

LWA